Here's My Heart, Here's My Hand

LIVING FULLY IN FRIENDSHIP WITH GOD

Other Books by William A. Barry, SJ

Contemplatives in Action:
The Jesuit Way (with Robert G. Doherty)

Finding God in All Things:
A Companion to the Spiritual Exercises of St. Ignatius

A Friendship Like No Other: Experiencing God's Amazing Embrace

God and You: Prayer as a Personal Relationship

God's Passionate Desire

A Hunger for God: Ten Approaches to Prayer

Letting God Come Close:
An Approach to the Ignatian Spiritual Exercises

Now Choose Life: Conversion as the Way to Life

Our Way of Proceeding: To Make the Constitutions of the Society of
Jesus and Their Complementary Norms Our Own

Paying Attention to God: Discernment in Prayer

The Practice of Spiritual Direction
(with William J. Connolly)

Seek My Face: Prayer as Personal Relationship in Scripture

Spiritual Direction and the Encounter with God:
A Theological Inquiry

What Do I Want in Prayer?

Who Do You Say I Am? Meeting the Historical Jesus in Prayer

With an Everlasting Love:
Developing an Intimate Relationship with God

Here's My Heart, Here's My Hand

LIVING FULLY IN FRIENDSHIP WITH GOD

William A. Barry, SJ

LOYOLAPRESS.
A JESUIT MINISTRY

Chicago

LOYOLA PRESS.
A JESUIT MINISTRY

3441 N. Ashland Avenue
Chicago, Illinois 60657
(800) 621-1008
www.loyolapress.com

Imprimi Potest: Very Reverend John J. Higgins, SJ, acting provincial

The Scripture quotations contained herein are from the New Revised Standard
Version Bible: Catholic Edition, copyright © 1993 and 1989 by the Division of
Christian Education of the National Council of the Churches of Christ in the U.S.A.
Used by permission. All rights reserved.

Original versions of chapters 1, 2, 3, 5, 10, 13, 16, and 18 appeared in *America*;
of chapters 6, 8, 9, 12, 14, and 15 in *Human Development*; of chapters 4, 5, and 17
in *Review for Religious*; and of chapter 11 in *The Tablet*. Permission to reprint is
gratefully acknowledged.

Cover photograph: Getty Images
Cover design by Rick Franklin
Interior design by Maggie Hong and Joan Bledig

Library of Congress Cataloging-in-Publication Data
Barry, William A.
  Here's my heart, here's my hand : living fully in friendship with God / William A.
Barry.
      p. cm.
  Includes bibliographical references.
  ISBN-13: 978-0-8294-2807-0
  ISBN-10: 0-8294-2807-0
  1. Spiritual life—Christianity. 2. Prayer—Christianity. 3. Spirituality. I. Title.
  BV4501.3.B375 2009
  248.4'82—dc22

                                                                    2008047379

Printed in the United States of America
09 10 11 12 13 14 Versa 10 9 8 7 6 5 4 3 2 1

To Peter-Hans Kolvenbach, SJ
with great gratitude, admiration, and affection

Contents

Introduction

He was praying in a certain place, and after he had
finished, one of his disciples said to him, "Lord, teach
us to pray." . . . "When you pray, say:

'Father, hallowed be your name.
Your kingdom come.
Give us each day our daily bread.
And forgive us our sins,
for we ourselves forgive everyone indebted to us.
And do not bring us to the trial.'" (Luke 11:1–4)

Jesus' response was short and sweet, but Christians down
the centuries do not seem to have been satisfied with these
simple words of advice. They have continually asked for
help with prayer, and thousands of fellow Christians have
been foolish enough to respond to their request. Mountains
of books have been produced in response to the simple
request, "Teach us to pray." None has matched the Master's
terseness and wisdom. But probably most of them, except
the ones trying to explain variants of what has come to be

called "centering prayer," just ring the changes on what Jesus taught. The Lord's Prayer is the model of all Christian prayer, after all is said and done.

But we can't seem to leave it at that, can we? You might have picked up this book because you were intrigued by the title and hoped, perhaps, that it would give you some help with your prayer. If you found this book in a bookstore, no doubt, there were a number of books on prayer for you to look at. Moreover, I have been writing about prayer for at least twenty-five years. In fact, the first versions of the chapters of this book appeared in various magazines over a period of about twenty years. Loyola Press believes that the hunger for books on prayer justifies publishing this one. What is going on? Why can't we accept Jesus' recipe for prayer and let it go at that?

I don't know the answer to those questions. I just know that I keep getting insights from my own prayer and from the experiences of people who talk with me about their prayer, and I feel the urge to publish them with the hope that others will find them helpful for their relationships with God. I get great consolation from hearing people talk about their relationship with God and from writing about God and God's desire for our friendship. So I keep on writing, even though I am aware that my basic insights are few and rather simple: God wants our friendship, and at the deepest level of our hearts all of us want what God wants; but our self-image, some rather faulty images of God, our resistance to letting God into our lives in any way but a superficial one, and many cares and worries hold us back from satisfying both of these desires. I keep playing variations on these themes, and so far enough people have been intrigued by what I write that I am encouraged to continue. So this is why you have this book in your hands.

As I mentioned, the book is a collection of chapters based on articles that appeared in various magazines over a period of years. All of the articles have something to do with prayer as a conscious relationship with God and the effects of engaging in this conscious relationship. Because the audiences of the articles were diverse, I have worked all of the articles over to try to give the whole book a somewhat congruent style, a conversational one. I want to engage you in a dialogue even though we cannot meet face-to-face. I write, at times, as though I am absolutely sure of myself. Don't be fooled by that tone. Sometimes, only half smilingly, I wonder whether I am trying to convince myself. Only a complete fool would be absolutely sure of anything he or she said about God. I am writing from my convictions, but I don't think I'm a fool. However, these are only my convictions, and God is always greater than anything I or anyone else can think. You need to read with an eye to your own experience and insight. So I mean my queries to the reader as the kind of question I would like to ask you if we were face-to-face.

As far as I am concerned, this book would be a failure if it did not, at least sometimes, cause you to want to argue with me about something I wrote. At times I have argued with myself. After all, some of the things I have learned about God in relation to me have run counter to ideas I thought were doctrinally absolute. The most obvious example is the notion of friendship with God. How could God, who is eternal, unchangeable, all knowing, all sufficient, ever be my friend? So if what I write touches a nerve in you, don't push it aside. Take it seriously and ask God whether what I write is true. I am writing not to prove that I'm correct about God or to give you good ideas, but to encourage you to engage in a close relationship with God. And even disagreements with the ideas of this book can serve that relationship.

I have organized the book along these lines: The first part takes up some of my ideas on prayer and how God communicates with us. You might find these chapters intriguing as they invite you to pay attention to your own experience as the privileged place where you meet God. In the second part I take up questions of how we decide what comes from God in our experience and what does not, traditionally known as the discernment of spirits. Perhaps you will be helped to discover how God is leading you in your life by reflecting on these chapters and your own experience. The third part has three meditations that may help you to live more comfortably with the dilemmas that the present plight of our world and church pose. In the fourth part you will find three meditations on who God is and what God wants in creating. Does what I write ring true to your experience? If not, you have something to discuss with God. The fifth part contains some meditations on how engaging with God changes us.

I encourage you to use the book not just for the sake of gaining more knowledge but also for the sake of improving your friendship with God. One way to do this is to read each chapter prayerfully, stopping periodically to talk with God about what you are reading, thinking, and feeling. If you find yourself engaged with God, just put the book aside and enjoy the conversation. Pick it back up again only when that conversation has ended. And remember Jesus' response to the request, "Teach us to pray." Basically, he said, "Talk to God as to your Creator who cares about you more than you'll ever know."

PART I

On Prayer

✧

In this part we will look at some questions that come up about prayer. I hold that God wants our friendship. Prayer, then, is a way to engage in this relationship of friendship with God. I hope that these meditations will help your prayer life.

✧

1

Why Do You Pray?

Someone might ask, "Why do you pray?" Let me be honest. At one time I prayed because I was a Jesuit. In other words, my answer meant, "I'm supposed to pray." Prayer was an obligation and, to be frank, a burden. At times I have prayed to placate God, to get God off my back, as it were. Many times I have prayed to obtain something, a favor, for example. Such answers to the question make prayer utilitarian. No doubt, my motivation for prayer still has vestiges of these answers. However, in my better moments my answer to the question now is, "I pray because I believe in God." Let me explain. In the process I hope that I will also say something helpful about how to pray.

What Does God Want?

Why did God create this universe? Let's play with the image of the garden in the second and third chapters of the book of Genesis. The image becomes clear after the sin of the first man and woman. We read: "They heard the sound of the LORD God walking in the garden at the time of the evening breeze, and the man and his wife hid themselves from the presence of the LORD God among the trees of the garden. But the LORD God called to the man, and said to him, 'Where are you?' He said, 'I heard the sound of you in the garden, and I was afraid, because I was naked; and I hid myself'" (Genesis 3:8–10).

If you sit with this image for a while, you realize that the author sees the earth as a garden in which God and human beings engage in daily work and get together in the evening to pass the time of day, perhaps to talk over the day. Before their sin the man and woman were unafraid before God; the fact that they are naked and show no shame symbolizes their transparency. This image speaks to my heart, and I hope that it will speak to yours. It tells us something about God's dream for our world.

God wants a world in which we work in harmony with God's intention in creation; a world in which God is active and we are active; a world in which, indeed, we cooperate with God in developing the planet. God wants us to be friends and partners in this creation. Sin throws a spanner into the works. Human beings act contrary to God's intention and become ashamed and afraid of God. The relationship of intimacy is broken.

The next few chapters of Genesis depict the consequences of human sin. Cain kills his brother Abel; human beings die at a younger and younger age; incest and other abominations follow; finally in chapter 11 human beings lose the ability to communicate with one another at the Tower of Babel. Yet God does not give up.

Chapter 12 of the Book of Genesis begins the story of God's efforts to bring us back into right relationship. God calls Abram and Sarai, from whom will come the chosen people, a people chosen not just for themselves but also to be light for the world. You can read the chapters that follow as a story of growing intimacy between God and Abram and Sarai, an intimacy signaled by the fact that God changes their names to Abraham and Sarah. In other words, the reversal of the catastrophe of human sin comes about by the recovery of an intimate relationship with God, a relationship in which human beings once again are asked to become partners with God. God chooses Abraham and Sarah, and through them the Israelites, to be the carriers of God's dream for the reversal of the effects of sin. The culmination of this choice of Israel, of course, is the appearance of Jesus of Nazareth. We who are followers of Jesus are to be the light of the world by living his way of intimacy and partnership with God.

So the God we believe in wants a relationship of intimacy and partnership with each of us and with all of us together. He wants us to be one family. If this is true, then God's creative desire, which brings the whole universe and each one of us into existence, touches us in the depths of our hearts. We are made for union with God, and our hearts must want that union at a very deep level. Augustine wrote: "You have made us for yourself, and our hearts find no peace until they rest in You" (*Confessions* I, 1). Julian of Norwich echoes the same idea: ". . . for our natural wish is to have God, and God's good wish is to have us, and we can never stop wanting or longing until we fully and joyfully possess him, and then we shall wish for nothing more" (*Revelations of Divine Love*, 1998, 50).

Why Pray?

Why do I pray? I pray because I believe in this God. Not only that, I pray because my heart aches for God even though I am also often afraid of closeness with God. I have met a lot of people who express this longing for God and who pray because they believe in the God who attracts them so much.

How to Pray?

This brings us to the question of how to satisfy this longing for God. The simplest answer is to engage in prayer. Here is where the hope that I might have something useful to say about how to pray comes into play. If God wants a friendship and partnership with each of us (and with all of us as a people), and we have a reciprocal desire for such a relationship, then prayer is similar to what happens in any friendship. Friendship between two people develops through mutual self-revelation. So in prayer I try to let God know who I am and ask that God do the same for me. It's that simple. As with Abraham and Sarah, it's a matter of growing mutual transparency. As we grow in our trust in God, we reverse the results of the sin of Adam and Eve. We are not ashamed to be naked before God, that is, to be open with all our thoughts, feelings, and desires.

Of course, even in human relationships what seems so simple can become very complex and difficult because of our fears and insecurities. So in our relationship with God fears and insecurities can get in the way. We may feel that we are not worthy of God's attention and love. It may be true, of course, that we are not worthy of God's love, but God doesn't seem to care. God loves us anyway, freely, and, it seems, with reckless abandon. So our fears are, in fact, groundless. However, we have to grow out of these fears, and the only way to do so is to engage in the relationship with God and find out for ourselves that God is hopelessly in love with us.

In principle, then, prayer is a simple thing. I tell God what is going on in my life and in my heart and wait for God's response. The psalms are examples of this kind of prayer. In them the psalmists tell God everything that is going on in their hearts, even things that we shudder to say. In Psalm 42 the psalmist tells God how much he longs for God. Psalm 104 praises God for the beauties of creation. Psalm 23 speaks of trust in God even in a dark hour. Psalm 51 begs God to pardon sins. Psalm 13 pleads angrily with God: "How long, O LORD? Will you forget me forever?" The beautiful Psalm 137 ends with this chilling prayer against the Babylonians: "Happy shall they be who take your little ones and dash them against the rock."

These psalmists let it all hang out in prayer. The psalms also record God's communication to the psalmists and to the people. For example, in Psalm 40: "I waited patiently for the LORD; he inclined to me and heard my cry. / He drew me up from the desolate pit." In other words, the psalmist experienced God's presence as a lifting of spirit in a hard time. And in Psalm 50: "Hear, O my people, and I will speak, O Israel, I will testify against you. I am God, your God. / Not for your sacrifices do I rebuke you." Prayer is a simple thing, but it requires a growing trust that God really wants to know everything about us, even those things that seem unsavory, and that God wants to reveal God's own self to us.

The Effects of Such Prayer

What happens when we pray in this way? Just as two friends change because of their deepening intimacy, so too a deepening intimacy with God changes us. But the change comes about through the relationship itself, not through sheer willpower. As we relate to God in this way, we become more like God. This is what happens in human relationships, is it not? We become like our best friends in our likes and dislikes, in our hopes and desires, and so on. So too we become like God through the kind of prayer indicated. We become like what we love.

The best way to become like God is to grow in our knowledge and love of Jesus of Nazareth, God in human flesh. When making the full Spiritual Exercises of Ignatius of Loyola, I come to a point at which I desire to know Jesus more intimately, to love him more, and to follow him more closely. But I can know another person only if that person reveals him- or herself to me. So my desire to know Jesus more intimately is a desire for Jesus to reveal himself to me. If I have this desire, I must, then, take time with the Gospels to let them stimulate my imagination so that Jesus can reveal himself—that is, reveal his dreams and hopes, his loves and hates, his hopes for me. As I engage in this kind of prayer, I will be surprised by what I discover about Jesus and thus about God, and about myself. In the process, I will come to love Jesus and become more like him.

Why do I pray? Because I believe in God, who loves us with an everlasting love and wants us as partners and friends. I pray, in other words, because God has made me for it.

You will find references to some helpful books on prayer as a relationship in the section "Recommended Readings" at the end of the book.

2

Does God Communicate with Me?

"You say that God wants to engage in a relationship of friendship with each of us and indicate that God communicates with us. I don't hear God speaking to me." I can imagine someone responding in this way to the first chapter of this book. I want to answer as best I can the question, "Does God communicate with me?"

In the first chapter I argued that God creates the world to invite each one of us into a relationship of intimacy, of friendship, of mutuality. If this is true, then God is always making overtures to us, is always communicating with each of us. So the answer to the question that the title of this chapter poses is yes, and the real question should be, "How do I pay attention to God's communication?" God, the creator of the universe, is not the god of the deists, one who created the world and then left it to carry on by itself much as a clockmaker makes a watch. God is always at work in this universe, aiming to bring about the divine intention in creating it, calling us to intimacy and friendship with God and with one another. So the question becomes, "How does God communicate with me or with anyone?"

Experiencing God's Desire for Us

When we are attracted to anyone or anything, the existing beauty of that person or thing draws us. But we do not exist until God desires us into existence. In desiring us, God creates us and makes us desirable to God and to others and desirous of God. God's action of desiring us into existence is not a once-and-for-all act in the past; it is ongoing, ever present. At every moment of our existence we are being created by God's desire for us. Do we experience this creative desire of God? I believe so. Every so often we are almost overcome by a desire for we know not what, for the all, and, at the same time, are filled with a sense of well-being. At these moments, I believe, we are experiencing God's creative desire for us and our own corresponding desire for God. God is the object of this desire for we know not what, for the all, for what we cannot even name.

In Anne Tyler's novel *Dinner at the Homesick Restaurant* we find a description of such an experience. An old, blind woman, Pearl Tull, has her son read from her childhood diary. It seems that before she dies, she wants to remember the experience she wrote about long ago:

> Early this morning I went out behind the house to weed. Was kneeling in the dirt by the stable with my pinafore a mess and perspiration rolling down my back, wiped my face on my sleeve, reached for the trowel, and all at once thought, Why I believe that at just this moment I am absolutely happy. The Bedloe girl's piano scales were floating out her window . . . and a bottle fly was buzzing in the grass, and I saw that I was kneeling on such a beautiful green little planet. I don't care what else might come about, I have had this moment. It belongs to me (1983, 284).

Over and over again I have found that people respond positively when I ask whether they have had experiences like this. These are experiences of God's communication to us. How about you? Can you recall experiences like this?

Once when I was discussing such experiences with a class of graduate students, an Australian sister spoke up. She had had such experiences, but she had also had experiences that were different. She had worked in the inner city of one of Australia's large cities. Often in the evening, after an exhausting day, she would take time for prayer and would be overcome by sobs of deep sorrow. In the quiet that followed, I asked her whether she would want to have more such experiences. She said, "Yes, but not only those." In the class there was a deep silence. I believed then, and still believe now, that she had experienced God's sorrow at what we have done to this "beautiful green little planet." I have come to believe that when we spontaneously experience great sorrow and compassion for another human being, we are experiencing God's own compassion.

Examples from the Prophets

The prophet Hosea fell helplessly in love with a prostitute and continued to love her in spite of her continued infidelity. As he pondered his own passionate love, he must have been astonished at himself. Perhaps reflecting on his experience he realized that he was experiencing some of God's own pathos over faithless Israel. When we really love and forgive someone who has done us wrong, I believe, we are experiencing God's love and forgiveness. Once I heard a talk by the Jesuit spiritual writer and spiritual director David Fleming. He maintained that when we pray, in the first week of the Spiritual Exercises, for shame and confusion because of our sins and the sinful condition of our world, we are asking to experience Jesus' shame and confusion as a human being for what human beings have done to other human beings, to the planet, to God. In other words, we are asking to experience God's shame and confusion over us sinners.

The prophet Micah puts these poignant words of complaint in God's mouth: "O my people, what have I done to you? In what have I wearied you? Answer me!" (6:3). The Creator of the universe begs his people for an answer, almost as though puzzled and ashamed at what they have done. This sounds like the shame and confusion that Ignatius has the retreatant pray for. Perhaps when we experience such shame and confusion at our own sins and at the horrors our fellow human beings perpetrate, we are experiencing God's communication to us. How do these ideas strike you?

The Experience of Compassion for Others

In my life I have met people of tremendous compassion for others. One is a pastoral care worker in a hospital who is often moved to tears of compassion for suffering patients. Her heart is nearly broken by the suffering of these strangers who become her family. Another is a man whose wife suffered from a brain disease that changed her personality. He told me how he loved her so much and how his heart was broken that she no longer knew how much he loved her. When I hear of experiences like these, tears well up in my eyes; I feel an awe and warmth that convinces me that I am in the presence of God, a God who loves others through the hearts of these people. When we experience compassion for others who are suffering, we are experiencing God's compassion. God is communicating to us and through us to the other.

Spontaneous Generosity

Once I acted generously without premeditation. In fact, as I thought about it later, it was an act of spontaneous generosity that I could not take credit for. I had been planning to use a gift certificate for some books for myself when, at lunch, I asked an elderly Jesuit if he could use some classical CDs. I do not know where this idea came from, but when he said that he would like some of Beethoven's symphonies, I went out and used the gift certificate for them. While I was doing this, I never thought of myself as generous; in fact, I did not think of myself at all. This is not my usual way of acting, as you can tell by the fact that I was surprised by it. I believe that I experienced God's generosity pouring out of me.

This incident reminded me of an experience that Frederick Buechner recorded in his memoir *The Sacred Journey*. He had just signed the contract for his first novel. As he left the publisher's office, he ran into a college classmate who was working as a messenger boy. Instead of feeling any pride that he had succeeded while this classmate had not, he felt a sadness, even shame, and realized, as he writes, "that, in the long run, there can be no real joy for anybody until there is joy finally for us all." He says that he can take no credit for this insight or this feeling. "What I felt was something better and truer than I was, or than I am, and it happened, as perhaps all such things do, as a gift" (1982, 97). When we are surprised by feelings, desires, and insights that are "something better and truer than" we are, perhaps we are experiencing God's presence drawing us into union with God and with all others.

Pay Attention to Your Experience

What I am suggesting is that we pay attention to our experience as the privileged place where God communicates to us. Our God is actively involved in this world and with each of us. God has a purpose in creating the universe and each of us; that purpose neither rests nor grows weary. If this is true, then we are the objects of God's communication at every moment of our existence. God is always knocking at our door, as it were. We are just not aware enough of the time. But we can grow in awareness if we wish. When we begin to pay more attention, we will discover that God's communication often shows itself in those times when we forget ourselves and are concerned with the other, whether that other is something in nature or another human being.

While Jesus was explaining the Scriptures to the disciples on the road to Emmaus, their hearts were burning (Luke 24:32), but they did not pay attention to this until after the breaking of bread. Even though they did not notice the burning of their hearts, they were caught up in the words of this stranger and thus were experiencing God's communication. When they recalled the experience, they recognized what had been happening on the road. We need to take time to look back over our day to see where our hearts were burning. We may well find that we have been touched often during a day by God. Yes, God does communicate to each one of us. Have the examples in this chapter reminded you of similar experiences of your own?

3

How Do I Know It's God?

I can hear someone who read the previous chapter asking, perhaps with some pique, "You tell me to pay attention to my experience as the privileged place where God communicates to me. But how do I know it's God who is communicating with me? Couldn't it just be wish fulfillment or even just good digestion that makes me feel treasured by God?" Readers of this book, like myself, live in a culture that is immersed in psychological explanations for every kind of experience; indeed, a culture that distrusts religious claims. How can we know whether we are experiencing God and not just ourselves and our own projections? In our age this is a burning question, but it was also a burning one at the time of Ignatius of Loyola. In his *Spiritual Exercises* he develops rules, the rules for the discernment of spirits, for answering such a question. It is rather astounding that a set of rules formulated by a man who lived more than four hundred years ago could still have relevance, yet many people are finding them a help to answer the question, "How do I know it's God?"

The Example of Ignatius

Ignatius himself began to learn how to tell God's influence from other influences during his long convalescence from a battle wound. He engaged in long daydreams of doing great deeds as a knight to win the favor of a great lady, a lady so great that, it seems, he had no realistic hope of winning her. He enjoyed the daydreams immensely. However, in the absence of the romantic novels he would have preferred, he began to read the life of Christ and a book of the lives of saints. His reflections on this reading led him to equally unrealistic daydreams; he imagined himself doing even greater deeds than these saints did for the love of Christ. Again, he enjoyed the daydreams immensely. There was a difference, however, but for a long time he did not notice it. After the daydreams about knightly deeds he felt sad and listless, whereas after those of imitating the saints he still felt joyful and alive. One day, he said, the light dawned, and he realized that God was communicating to him through one set of daydreams, the ones that inspired continuing joy, whereas the "bad spirit" was behind the other daydreams, the ones that left him sad afterward.

Note well: Ignatius was not praying when he made this first discernment of God's communication; he was daydreaming. Moreover, both sets of daydreams had a quality of narcissistic, unrealistic ambition to them. Yet he came to believe that God used one set of such daydreams to draw him toward a new way of life. Because of experiences like these Ignatius came to believe that God is always communicating to us, that every experience has a touch of God in it. It is almost a motto of Ignatian spirituality that God can be found in all things. The only question is whether or not we will be aware of God's presence.

So how did Ignatius figure out that God was communicating with him in this case? He finally paid attention to his emotional states during and after the two sets of daydreams. During both he felt elated and excited, but after the daydreams of doing great knightly deeds, he felt sad and listless, while after the daydreams of following Christ, he still felt elated. The first lesson in discerning how God communicates, then, is to pay attention to our experiences and to the emotional states that our experiences arouse. The second lesson, strange to say, is that Ignatius discovered God's presence through feeling happy and excited; strange to say, because we may not often associate feeling happy and excited with God's presence. For the rest of this chapter I want to paraphrase the first two rules for the discernment of spirits that Ignatius formulated in the *Spiritual Exercises*.

Some Rules of Thumb for Discernment

The first rule of thumb is that one look at one's ordinary orientation with regard to God and to one's life as a Christian. Do I try to lead a good Christian life insofar as possible? Or am I playing fast and loose with how I know I should be living? As an example of the latter, think of an owner of a grocery store who regularly cheats his customers through small weight changes in his packaging. Suppose that he were to try to engage in a relationship with God. What do you think would happen? Probably he would begin to feel pangs of conscience as he realized how good God has been to him and recalled his cheating. He might feel some relief from these pangs of conscience with thoughts like these: "It's small potatoes, just an ounce or two in each package. And my volume is small. I know that large chains make huge profits." Ignatius would say that the pangs of conscience come from God and that the rationalizations that give relief come from the evil spirit or from the grocer's own unwillingness to change his lifestyle.

What about the person who is trying to live a decent Christian life, even if not perfectly, say, a working mother and wife who tries her best to do an honest day's work and to take care of her family obligations? One such person felt great joy and peace in God's presence and looked forward to prayer. Soon, however, she experienced anxiety, feeling that she was being too proud to expect God to speak to her and that taking time for prayer like this was a luxury she could ill afford. She said to herself, "This is too highfalutin for the likes of me." God now seemed distant. Ignatius would say that the positive experiences come from God or the good spirit who wants to draw her into friendship, whereas the troubling thoughts come from the bad spirit or from her fears of closeness to God.

So the first rule of thumb urges us to establish the general orientation of our lives. If I am out of synch with God in my life, I can expect that God will try to get me to change my life; I will feel pangs of conscience or concerns about certain aspects of my life. These pangs of conscience, however, will not lead to anxious, scrupulous examinations of all my motivations; they will gently point out where I have gone wrong. The bad spirit or my own desire not to face a change will whisper blandishments in my ear to convince me that all is OK. An example from my own life: for some time I had had concerns about the amount of alcohol I was drinking and how it was affecting my health. I rationalized them away because I was functioning quite well in daily life. However, I was often sleepy in the evening after dinner when I wanted to pray. One day, because of the intervention of a friend, I realized that the concerns about my drinking were from God. I was given the grace to stop drinking and have been much happier for it. God's communication came in the form of the nagging concerns that wanted to lead me to a happier and healthier life.

On the other hand, if we are trying to live in tune with God's intention, says Ignatius, God will console us, help us to move forward, encourage us in our efforts to live a good life. But the bad spirit or our own fears of closeness to God will try to make us leery of developing a closer relationship with God, as happened with the woman mentioned previously. Ignatius, for example, had the thought at one point after his conversion: "And how will you be able to put up with this (namely, his ascetical life and prayers) for the seventy years you have ahead of you?" Ignatius quite rightly answered that no one could guarantee that he would live for even one more day.

The second rule of thumb follows from the first. God wants us to be happy and fulfilled. But the only way we can be happy and fulfilled is to be in tune with God's desire for the world and for us. For those who are trying to lead a life in tune with God's intention, consolation is the order of the day for the most part. This does not mean that life will be without pain and suffering; it means that God wants to be a consoling presence to us even in the inevitable pains and sufferings life has in store. If this is true, then the terrible mental agony and torture scrupulous people go through is not from God. After all, scrupulous people are trying to live in tune with God. Ignatius himself, during the early days after his conversion, was plagued by scruples; he feared that he had not confessed all his sins. Things got so bad that he contemplated suicide. Yet at this point in his life he was trying with great fervor, indeed excessive fervor, to live a life in accordance with God's dream. He finally came to the conclusion that these scrupulous thoughts could not be from God. In other words, he finally realized that God wanted his peace and happiness, not torture of his mind and soul.

Do these two rules make sense to you? What I am saying is rather simple. We can discern, in our experience, what is from God from what is not from God. But to do so, we have to believe that God is communicating with us and that we do experience God's communication. As Christians we are committed to faith in God as the Mystery who is always trying to draw each of us and all of us together, into friendship. Now we need to put that faith into practice by taking seriously our experience. One way to do this is to engage in the exercise Ignatius calls the daily examination of conscience. At some point in the day we stop for a few minutes to ask for God's help to go back over the experience of the part of the day just concluded. After a moment of gratitude to God we go back over the events of the day so far. What stands out? What affected us most deeply? What troubled us? Such a look back over the day can lead to a conversation with God about our reactions. It can also lead us to use these rules of thumb to try to see how God was communicating to us and how we responded. We can, indeed, know God's voice.

PART II

On Discernment and Decision Making

❖

In part I we began to look at the question of how to discern what is of God in our experience from other influences. In this part I will offer some meditations on discernment and on decision making in the Ignatian tradition with the hope that they will spark insight and help you to attune your life with God's dream.

❖

4

God's Love Is Not Utilitarian

In the first chapter I mentioned that God's love does not seem to have a utilitarian purpose. Here I want to reflect with you on the realization that God does not love us for some extraneous reason—for example, so that we will carry out some plan God has for our part of our world. I maintain that God's love does not have a utilitarian purpose.

A number of years ago —more than I care to remember—as a brash, young Jesuit in training I was engaged in a spirited conversation with some other Jesuits. We were discussing the reasons for being a Jesuit. During the discussion I found myself more and more dissatisfied with the reasons given, most of which revolved around the idea that the vow of chastity made us more available for service. I had seen married and single men and women who were at least as dedicated to being followers of Christ as any of us. My own parents were examples of rather remarkably unselfish lovers. I could not believe that God was more pleased with us than with them. Nor could I accept the notion that God wanted me to be a Jesuit to save some part of the world. That just did not ring true to my experience and reflection.

At one point I blurted out something like this: "I'm a Jesuit because God wants me to be happy and productive. God's love for me has led me to choose this life, just as his love for others leads them to choose their way of life." I did not understand all the implications of what I said, nor was I sure that the implied theology would stand up to scrutiny. But that outburst has stayed with me through the years, and I have pondered its meaning off and on. In the process I began to enunciate a conviction that God's love is not utilitarian; that is, God does not love me or anyone else primarily to achieve some other goals. In this meditation I want to unpack some of the meaning of this conviction, impelled by a number of experiences directing retreats and giving spiritual direction.

My youthful outburst was occasioned by the realization that much of the reasoning that justified belonging to a religious congregation presumed that joining it involved great sacrifice. So the life had to be justified or made palatable. But I did not feel that my life entailed any more sacrifice than anyone else's. I was rather happy, all things considered, and would not have traded my life for anyone's. So I felt that the call to Jesuit life was God's gift to me, God's way of loving me. To put the same thing in another way: I felt that God wanted me to be a Jesuit because that was the best way for me to be happy and productive. That conviction has not changed since.

What Does God Want of Us?

Over the years I have come to believe that all God wants of any us is to love and befriend us. I also believe that it is very difficult for us to let God love us, to receive love. We resist God's overtures of love and invitations to friendship rather strongly. I have probed some of the sources of that resistance in three chapters of *Paying Attention to God*. Here I want to focus on what I have come believe is God's desire in our regard.

In *Let This Mind Be in You* Sebastian Moore notes that God's desire creates us. God desires us into existence, and thus we become desirable and lovely to God. Moreover, God wants us to discover the divine loveliness and let ourselves be attracted to it. But this can happen only if we ourselves believe and experience that we are the apple of God's eye— to the extent that we believe and experience that God finds us desirable, to that extent will we be in love with God.

People who have let God demonstrate this kind of love for them often affirm that it is a love without any demands, without any strings attached. This is a difficult point to grasp, so let us try to be clear. Often enough we are afraid of God's closeness because we fear the demands that will be made: "God may ask me to go to Ethiopia." As far as I can tell, when God comes close, a list of demands or conditions for continuing to remain close are not part of the deal. For example, God does not seem to say, "Yes, I love you, but I will keep on loving you only if you [fill in the blank]." In fact, God does not even seem to say, "I love you, but I will keep on loving you only if you stop this particular sin." God seems be just what the first letter of John says, namely, love, and unconditional love at that. All God seems to want is to be able to love us, to be close and intimate with us. Have you ever experienced God in this way?

Doesn't God Have Standards?

Does this mean that God has no standards, no values? By no means; but those who have let God come close do not perceive these values as demands. Rather, they find themselves desirous of sharing these values, of being like God—not because God demands that they do so, but because they are happier and more alive when they live according to God's values. For example, I realize that I am happier, more alive, and more purposeful when I want to forgive as Jesus forgives, to love as Jesus loves.

Married men and women have often found themselves most fulfilled when they have remained faithful to their marital commitments, even when the grass looked greener elsewhere. Men and women in religious congregations have discovered that their greatest happiness lies in giving themselves wholeheartedly to the demands of their vows, even when the bloom seems off the rose, as it were. Many Christians have also discovered that they are most alive and happy when they give themselves as wholeheartedly as possible to living with and working with and for the poor. Of course, at times all these people weaken, and some negative sanction helps them stay the course—for example, fear of loss of face or of sinning and disappointing God or of hell. But at bottom the motivation for sticking to their last is the desire to imitate God, who has so unconditionally and faithfully loved them. In other words they want to be perfect as their heavenly Father is perfect (Matthew 5:48). Does this make sense to you? Does it square with your experience?

Of course, none of us can do this. Sin is an ever-present reality with which even the holiest among us must contend. However, those who have experienced God as lover do not experience God as contemptuous of their sinfulness; rather, God comes across as compassionate and patient. In their best moments, when they are aware of God's love, they recognize that all they have to do is to ask forgiveness and healing for their lapses, and to desire to have their hearts made more like the heart of Jesus. And they can hope that continued contemplation of Jesus will transform their hearts almost by osmosis.

Jesus as the Key to Understanding God's Love

Now, perhaps, we have come to the key that opens the last door to insight. Jesus is the perfect human being, we believe, the one who most fully realizes the potential of humanity. When all is said and done, what is the central insight Jesus had? Was it not that YHWH, the Creator of the universe, the Unnameable, Unfathomable Mystery, is Abba, dear Father, dear Mother, Love itself? To the maximum extent possible for a human being Jesus knew God, and he experienced God as Love.

Let us reflect a bit on Jesus' baptism in the Jordan. I realize that I am reading into the text, but I find it intriguing that the Gospels picture God as telling Jesus, "You are my Son, the Beloved; with you I am well pleased" (Luke 3:22). This happens *before* Jesus has begun his public ministry. What has he done to elicit such praise? Perhaps "all" that he has done is to allow God to come as close as God wants to come; perhaps all that he has done is to let himself be loved as much as God wants to love him. Perhaps Jesus is so dear to God just because he let God do what God has always wanted to do: to be our lover par excellence.

It is also intriguing to speculate that Jesus' fundamental saving act may have been not dying on the cross but rather accepting God's love as much as it is humanly possible to do. Then the following of Christ might mean not so much doing heroic deeds, or even wanting to love as Jesus loves, but much more fundamentally desiring to let oneself be loved as much as Jesus was and is loved. Perhaps the world will be saved when there is a critical mass of people who deeply believe and experience how much God loves them.

Is This a "Me and God" Spirituality?

What I have been saying may strike some readers as advocacy of a "me and God" spirituality. It is true that in theory this can sound very narcissistic. But in practice, it is the exact opposite.

Those who let themselves be loved by God find in doing so that their own love and compassion for others increase enormously. This transformation does not happen because God demands such love of them. In fact, they know that for years they tried to be loving in response to what they took to be God's demands: they made resolution after resolution and failed miserably. Now, without effort almost, they find their hearts going out to others, and especially to the neediest. They are surprised themselves at what is happening to their hearts. The more they allow themselves to be loved unconditionally by God, the more loving they become. Have you noticed something like this in your own life or in the life of someone you know?

And the love of these people, like that of Jesus, is a tough love. They speak the truth, but it is a truth that is not contemptuous or angrily demanding—at least while they are aware of being loved. This last aside is a necessary nod to realism. For even the holiest saints have days they regret. In addition to speaking the truth, as they become or are made aware that they are sociopolitical beings—that is, constituted at least in part by the social and political institutions into which they are born or freely enter—they begin to take steps to make these institutions more just and caring through organizing, networking, lobbying, and protesting when necessary.

Moreover, people who let God come close realize, without self-contempt, how far they fall short and always will fall short of being like Jesus. They know from experience why the saints protested so strongly their sinfulness. They feel over and over again how much God loves them and how much God desires to shower them with love, and they see themselves turning away, resisting these advances, and refusing the invitation to intimacy. They find themselves to be enigmas because the experience of God's closeness fulfills their deepest desires, yet they fight this closeness off.

In spite of knowing how sinful they are, they also know that God still loves them. Hence, they view themselves and all human beings more and more with the compassionate eyes of God. Does this make sense to you? Have you felt some of these movements yourself or met people who act this way because of a growing friendship with God?

A Defense against Accepting God's Unconditional Love?

I have begun to suspect that the notion of God's love as utilitarian is a defense against accepting God's love. If I convince myself that God loves me for the sake of other people, then I do not have to face the enormity of being loved by God for myself alone. Many people shelter themselves from the full implications of God's love by seeing themselves as the object of that love only as part of a group. In other words, God loves all people, and I am included under the tent, as it were. Now there is a truth in this notion, but I can use it to keep God's love very impersonal and distanced.

So too, God is kept at a distance if I conceive of God's love for me as utilitarian: "God loves me for what I can do for others." It is a very subtle way of keeping God at a distance: "God does not love *me* so much as these other people." I am loved for what I can do for God. Interestingly enough, it is also a way both to puff up my ego and to make sure that I am never satisfied with myself. On the one hand, I am aware of all that I am doing for others; on the other hand, I am constantly reminded of how much more there is to be done, and I may also be reminded that others have done more. One person on a retreat, for example, felt that if God really loved her, then God would use her in more important ways. She discovered that such reasoning was making her unhappy and keeping God at arm's length.

Perhaps the burden of the argument thus far can be summed up by the example of a man on retreat. Peter had experienced deeply that Jesus knew he was a sinner and would always be a sinner. Jesus communicated in a gentle way that Peter had betrayed him in the past and that he would do it again in the future. Yet Jesus looked at him with enormous tenderness and love. Peter felt that Jesus said to him: "I love no one more than I love you, but I love no one less than I love you." God does not love some people more because of what they do or what they will do. God is just greatly pleased that people let this love into their lives.

Does It Matter What I Do Then?

If God's love is not utilitarian, does this mean that it is meaningless to ask whether God has a will for me apart from letting God love me and loving in return? If God will continue to love me whether I become a doctor, a carpenter, a social worker, or a Jesuit, does it matter at all to God what I become, as long as I am happy? To take the question one step further: if God will continue to love me even if I continue to sin, does it matter to God whether or not I stop sinning?

Perhaps John was addressing some of the same questions when he has Jesus say:

> For God so loved the world that he gave his only Son, so that everyone who believes in him may not perish but may have eternal life. Indeed, God did not send the Son into the world to condemn the world, but in order that the world might be saved through him. Those who believe in him are not condemned; but those who do not believe are condemned already, because they have not believed in the name of the only Son of God. And this is the judgment, that the light has come into the world, and people loved darkness rather than light because their deeds were evil. For all who do evil hate the light and do not come to the light, so that their deeds may not be exposed. But those who do what is true come to the light, so that it may be clearly seen that their deeds have been done in God. (John 3:16–21)

The great Scripture scholar Raymond Brown indicates that, while Jesus does not judge, his very presence does draw people to judge themselves. In other words, Jesus does not condemn, but his presence brings out what people really are like. He, the human presence of God on earth, loves people and wants their good, indeed their absolute good, which is union with God, and he continues to love even those who spurn the offer. They condemn themselves. Let us see where this path leads us.

When we love people unselfishly (insofar as this is possible for a human being), we want their good. We want them to be as happy, fulfilled, as right with God and the world as possible. We want them to fulfill all their potential. At our best we do not demand all this as a condition for our love, but we want it because we love them.

If this is the case with us, we can imagine what God wants. In his "Contemplation to Obtain Love," Ignatius of Loyola tries to help us to imagine all that God's love wants. In a poignant line he says: "I will ponder with great affection how much God our Lord has done for me, and how much he has given me of what he possesses, and finally, how much, as far as he can, the same Lord desires to give himself to me according to his divine decrees."

God creates a world that is "very good" (Genesis 1:31) for us loved ones to live in. God wants us to be cocreators of this evolving world. The Garden of Eden image in Genesis is a wonderful symbol of what God wants for all of us. God wants us to live in harmony with, and with reverence for, the universe and all that is in it, because that is the way to our greatest happiness and fulfillment both as individuals and as brothers and sisters.

Moreover, Ignatius writes, God wants to "give himself to me . . . as far as he can." The limitation comes not just from our finitude but also from our perversity. God, however, will not compel us to accept what is for our good.

What about Punishment for Sins?

Does God punish us for our perversity? An age-old tradition ascribes natural disasters to God's wrath. The Old Testament is filled with such statements, beginning with chapter 3 of the book of Genesis. In the New Testament Jesus is asked, "Rabbi, who sinned, this man or his parents, that he was born blind?" He answers, "Neither this man nor his parents sinned; he was born blind so that God's works might be revealed in him" (John 9:2–3). To say the least, this answer is enigmatic, but it does raise questions about ascribing disasters to God's wrath at sin.

On the hypothesis that God is love I want to say that we punish ourselves by turning away from God's love. God's love remains steadfast. But hatred, suspicion, prejudice, and fear—these and other states of mind—are the product of our sins and of the sins of our forebears. And they are not states of mind that are for our peace or for the peace of our world. In other words, God made us brothers and sisters and desired us to live in harmony and mutual love, but we human beings have brought on ourselves the disharmony and distrust that now threaten the world as we know it. And if anyone does remain willfully and perversely turned away from God's love and the love of neighbor to the end, then he or she chooses eternal unhappiness. But God's love does not change into something else.

But what about the man born blind? What about the child with Down syndrome? What about natural disasters such as the tsunami of 2004 that took hundreds of thousands of lives in one day? We want to know why such things happen.

It lies close to hand to ascribe such events to the punishment of God or fate or the stupidity of the victims. Social psychologists speak of the just-world hypothesis in describing such attitudes. People generally hold that we get what we deserve because it's too daunting to think otherwise. If bad things could happen to good and prudent people, then they could happen to me. So, operating with the just-world hypothesis, I look for the mistakes people made that have led to the disasters that have befallen them.

Some of these calamities may be caused by human sinfulness or stupidity at some time in history. In the United

States and in Latin America people still experience the effects of the evil of slavery and of greedy colonization. Other calamities may just be random events in a finite world, such as some of the effects of genetic disorders. Others may be caused by someone else's perversity, but the victim is seemingly picked out at random: for example, a drunken driver plows into John Jones's car, having just barely missed ten others, and suddenly John is dead and his daughter is maimed for life, through no fault of theirs. The just-world hypothesis reminds us of the friends of Job or the disciples who asked Jesus about the sin that caused the man to be born blind. It will not work in the case of innocent victims of random events, the present sins of others, or the effects of historical evils.

How do we square the unconditional love of God with such calamities? In experience, people who engage God directly in a relationship, and who look at the world realistically, have the just-world hypothesis pulled out from under them. They see that Jesus, the sinless, beloved Son, died horribly and that no bolts of lightning took vengeance on his killers or saved him. As they develop their relationship with God, they may find themselves raging at God because of the seemingly needless suffering they undergo or see others experience. Somehow or other they discover a God who is beyond what we conceive as justice, a God they can hope in and live for. No more than the author of the book of Job can they explain it; but for sure it is not the answer proposed by the just-world hypothesis.

People who have developed such a relationship with God experience the deep mystery of creation and cocreation. God loves into existence not only the stars that so bedazzle us in the night sky but also the volcano that erupts suddenly and engulfs a whole city killing twenty thousand people, and God loves those people into existence. God loves into existence not only Jesus and Mary, Francis of Assisi, Teresa of Ávila, and the lovely people who have loved us in our lives but also Herod and Herodias, Genghis Khan, Lucrezia Borgia, Adolf Hitler, and the torturers of political prisoners of our day. People who meet this God at a deep level sense a bottomless compassion and pain at the heart of the world, yet a vibrant hope for life. They become more compassionate and passionate themselves. Perhaps they now understand that it was not bravado that kept the martyrs joyful in their suffering and dying. Perhaps, too, they now understand how the poorest of the poor still are capable of tremendous acts of generosity toward their fellow sufferers, just as they can understand the great cruelty of which the poor are also capable.

Thus far we have threaded our path out of the seeming dilemma of the coexistence of God's unconditional love and punishment for sin and hell. We have also seen a way to explain the call to conversion from sin. God wants the best for us, and that best includes our turning away from sin and toward living a life that is consonant with a relationship of mutual love with the lord. Sin does not produce happiness or harmony or peace of mind. Nor does it create harmonious relationships between people or political and social and religious institutions that work toward such harmonious and just relationships. So God's love for us desires that we be converted to want and to work for what God wants. Note, however, that God does not make such conversion a condition for continuing to love us. God desires such conversion because it is for our good but does not demand it as the price of love. Am I making some sense to you?

What about Discernment of God's Will?

Now let us move on to the issue of the discernment of God's will, especially as this regards the question of a vocation to a way of life. Traditionally Catholics have believed that God has a plan for each person: God calls some to the religious or priestly life and others to the married state. Truth to tell, the term *vocation* was most often restricted to the religious or priestly life. "He has a vocation" was shorthand in Catholic circles for saying that an individual felt called to religious or priestly life. But a more careful use of language also saw married life as a calling. A further problem, of course, is that this language left in limbo those who remain single (and not religious or priests) either voluntarily or involuntarily. At any rate, does God call people to a particular way of life? And if so, how is this calling consonant with the non-utilitarian nature of God's love?

Again we return to the idea that the lover wants the good of the beloved. I will use the case of Ignatius of Loyola to illustrate a way to understand God's call in terms of love, without making that love utilitarian.

Ignatius was a hell-raising, ambitious, vain, courageous man, a man who dreamed of doing great exploits. At Pamplona, according to his own account, he was the rallying point in resisting the French attackers. When he was severely wounded in the leg, the defenders immediately surrendered. God seems to have used this crooked line to write straight. During his long convalescence, as I mentioned in the previous chapter, Ignatius gave himself to daydreams. He dreamed of doing great knightly deeds to win fame and honor and the favor of a great lady. These daydreams would absorb him for up to four hours at a time. After he read the only books at hand, a life of Christ and a book of the lives of the saints, he began to dream of doing what Dominic and Francis did, and again he would become absorbed for hours. Notice that in both cases his ardor, ambition, bravery, and even vanity were operative. Finally, after some time of alternating daydreams, he began to notice a difference. When he dreamed of doing great worldly deeds, he felt wonderful during them but listless and ill at ease afterward. But with the dreams of following Jesus he felt wonderful during and after them. This was the beginning of Ignatius's own discovery of the discernment of spirits, a discernment that eventually led him to found the Society of Jesus, with enormous consequences for the church and the world—and for not a few individuals who in almost 450 years have joined the Society.

How are we to understand this story of a vocation? I would maintain that God's love for Ignatius involved the desire that Ignatius use his great energies, his ardor, and his ambition in ways that would make him most happy, most fulfilled, and most useful to others. I believe that it mattered a great deal to God how Ignatius used his talents, for Ignatius's own sake first of all, but also for the sake of others whom God loved. However, God would not have loved Ignatius any the less if he had missed the opportunity for discernment and had continued on his course toward worldly achievement. But God might have been greatly saddened that Ignatius did not choose what was for his greater happiness and peace. Later in life Ignatius might have felt the sadness as he pondered how his life had gone since his recuperation. Only God could so love us as to allow us the freedom to turn away from receiving all that God wants to give us, and still keep loving us unconditionally, even when we so choose.

It seems to me that a consistent cleaving to the central insight of the New Testament, that God is our Abba, our dear Father, does not force us to give up any truths of faith and has several distinct advantages. The preceding pages have shown some ways of understanding traditional truths while holding in the forefront of our minds that God is unconditional love. Such an understanding demonstrates an intrinsic connection between the love of God and the search for God's will. Because God loves me, God wants the best for me. Because and insofar as I love God, I want the best for God, which seems to be that I accept God's love and live in tune with the kingdom Jesus preached.

The way of life God wants for me is the best way for me to receive God's love and to be a cocreator. Hence, in my better moments, I try to the best of my ability to discern where that love leads me. I do not try to find God's will for fear that I will be punished if I don't but rather for fear that I will miss the way that would allow God to give me more of God's self. I also try to find God's will because I know that God desires more good for all those whom I will touch in my life. Does this make sense to you? I hope so.

A Final Question

One final question occurs. Suppose that Ignatius's eyes had not opened up during his convalescence and that he had gone on to worldly exploits. Would he have been given another chance? That is, of course, an unanswerable question. But God would surely continue to love him and, we presume, continue to call him to a radical conversion of heart. If, later in life, he were to have his eyes opened, he might have to come to terms with those earlier missed opportunities. Repentance would be in order, but a wallowing in his spilt milk would not be an appropriate response to the God of love. Conversion means to accept my past precisely as my past, that is, both mine and past, and to surrender in freedom to the new and mysterious future offered by God's love now.

But a historic moment surely would have been lost if Ignatius had taken an alternative route instead of the one he did take. There are consequences to our choices. Hence, it is incumbent on all of us who stand before serious life choices to become discerning Christians. Historic consequences may be at stake.

We need to be mindful that there is a force within us that does hate the light, that seems to want to thwart all God's loving desire to give to us. We need to be on the alert to discern the presence of that force but also to rely on those various sayings that have given people hope through the ages, sayings like: "For mortals it is impossible, but not for God; for God all things are possible" (Mark 10:27), or "My grace is sufficient for you, for power is made perfect in weakness" (2 Corinthians 12:9).

5

The Kingdom of God and Discernment

If God's love does not have a utilitarian purpose, what does the kingdom of God that Jesus preached mean? Doesn't God want us to contribute to this kingdom? In the course of studying the biblical meaning of the phrase "the kingdom of God," I had an idea that may be of interest to readers and a spur to your discernment of how to live in tune with God.

New Testament scholars have agreed that the centerpiece of Jesus' preaching was the kingdom or reign of God, but it is not so easy to know what Jesus understood by the phrase. Kenneth Leech, in *Experiencing God: Theology as Spirituality*, believes that the facts can best be understood by a series of negations. First, the kingdom of God in the New Testament is not an otherworldly hope, a heaven peopled by the souls of the saved. When Jesus says, "My kingdom is not of this world," he does not mean that it is or will be located someplace else but that its origins and values are from God and are immanent (in this world) only as transcendent (not of this world). Indeed, when they become immanent, they are met with opposition and struggle precisely because they are not of this world.

Second, the kingdom of God is not seen as a gradual, evolutionary movement. Suddenness and surprise are more the flavor of Jesus' parables of the kingdom. One gets the sense that people will be shocked when they find out what God's reign means and who actually accepts that reign, much as Mrs. Turpin in Flannery O'Connor's short story "Revelation" is shocked by her vision of a vast swinging bridge:

> Upon it a vast horde of souls were rumbling toward heaven. There were whole companies of white-trash, clean for the first time in their lives, and bands of black niggers in white robes, and battalions of freaks and lunatics shouting and clapping and leaping like frogs. And bringing up the end of the procession was a tribe of people whom she recognized at once as those who, like herself and Claud, had always had a little of everything and the God-given wit to use it right. . . . They were marching behind the others with great dignity, accountable as they had always been for good order and common sense and respectable behavior.

> They alone were on key. Yet she could see by their
> shocked and altered faces that even their virtues were
> being burned away. (*The Complete Stories*, 1987, 508)

Third, the kingdom of God is not an individual, inner experience having nothing to do with anyone else. It is, of course, an inner experience, but an experience that depends on community and tends toward the forming of community.

Fourth, the kingdom of God is not wholly future. It is both present and future. In Jesus' preaching the kingdom of God is now as well as not yet.

Finally, it must be emphasized that the kingdom of God is not the same as the church. The church proclaims the kingdom and is a sacrament of the kingdom, but it is not the kingdom itself. Nor is membership in the church as such a guarantee of being finally under the reign of God.

Put positively, then, the kingdom or reign of God is immanent in this universe, yet transcendent; it is present and not yet present; it is and will be experienced as a surprising and disturbing presence; it is immanent in individuals but only as part of a community; and it is only presaged by the church while yet being present in the church. In truth, the kingdom of God seems to bear all the characteristics of God, the Creator and Lord of the universe, who is both transcendent to and immanent in the universe and who is experienced by individuals in a community.

Given this understanding of the kingdom of God, it is obvious that we do not build up or even help to build up the kingdom. God alone effects God's reign, or to put it even more strongly, God alone is God, the reign of God. The question is, "Do we have any role to play?"

God's Desire

Although the kingdom of God is equated with God, there would be no need of such a concept if there were no created universe. We can understand the kingdom of God as God's intention for the universe, or rather as God's one action that is the universe. The latter phrase is borrowed from John Macmurray's Gifford Lectures of 1953 and 1954 (*The Self As Agent* and *Persons in Relation*). According to Macmurray, any action of a person is guided by an intention. For example, I intended to write this book. That intention makes the writing of the book with all that went into it one action. I am immanent in this one action, but I am also transcendent to it. I express myself, but I am not the book. So too, Macmurray argues, one can only think of the universe as God's one action informed by one intention. Rowan Williams, the present archbishop of Canterbury, writes in *On Christian Theology* of God's creative action: "What God utters . . . is God: the summons to the world to be, and to find its fruition in being in the presence of God, sets 'outside' God the kind of life that is God's" (2000, 73–74). Just as we humans are immanent in, yet transcendent to our actions, so too, and *a fortiori*, is God. God's one action includes all of the events (things that just happen) and actions (things that persons do) that constitute the history of the universe.

Just as you cannot know the intentions of my action unless I reveal them, *a fortiori*, we cannot know God's intention unless God reveals it. Even then we will know only darkly and by faith. So the question is, "Has God revealed the divine intention for the universe?" At the least we can say that God has revealed that intention for our world, whatever may be said of the whole universe. This intention, it seems, is that all human beings live as brothers and sisters in a community of faith, hope, and love, united with Jesus Christ as sons and daughters of God our Father and in harmony with the whole created universe: "Blessed be the God and Father of our Lord Jesus Christ" who "has made known to us the mystery of his will, according to his good pleasure that he set forth in Christ, as a plan for the fullness of time, to gather up all things in him, things in heaven and things on earth" (Ephesians 1:3, 9–10).

This notion of the universe as God's one action seems to coincide with the characteristics of the kingdom of God enumerated earlier. It is immanent, yet transcendent; it is this-worldly, yet is an action of God; it is a surprising and even shocking presence because it includes the whole world and demands the breakdown of all sectarian and national divisions; it is experienced only in community and, in fact, is not yet realized as long as any individual or group is in principle excluded from the community; it is quite obviously not simply equated with the church—even if the church is conceived as the union of all Christian churches—because God's one action includes the whole world and all its people.

Our Role in What God Desires

But the question of our role in this one action of God must still be addressed. If we do not build up the kingdom of God—that is, if we do not build up or create the one action God intends—what do we do or what can we do? If the universe is one action of God, then our own actions can be in tune with this one action or not. Insofar as our actions are in tune, we are satisfied and fulfilled; insofar as they are not, we are and will be frustrated in our intentions. In other words, God's one intention will be achieved because God is God. We can be more or less satisfied in life depending on whether and how well we are in tune with God's one action. And insofar as we are in tune, the kingdom of God is immanent in us. To the extent that we are in tune with God's one action, our actions by God's grace intend the community of all people and try to let that community emerge. We try, with God's grace and in the concrete circumstances of our lives, to cooperate with others to overcome fears and hatreds and to create an atmosphere and social institutions in which men and women are enabled to live together as brothers and sisters.

That is our role. To be fulfilled and deeply happy in this life we need to let our hearts become attuned to the one action of God, to let God's intention for our world guide our actions. Prayer, disciplined reflection, and discernment, then, are urgently needed, not to build up the kingdom but to know where it is, how we should fit into it, and for us to be truly happy. Traditionally spiritual writers have spoken of discernment as finding God's will. If we take the will of God as the intention that informs God's one action in creation, we may, perhaps, be able to broaden our understanding of what discernment means.

Discernment of God's Desire for Us

First of all, Christians who have not yet made a commitment to a way of life in the church (the vocations of marriage, religious life, priesthood, lay ministry, missionary work, or a profession, for example) have the opportunity to discern which way of life for them is most in tune with God's one action, given their temperament, talents, upbringing, societal constraints, and previous choices in life. The question of discernment comes down

to which way of life is most fulfilling, challenging, and satisfying for me, because the more I am in tune with God's one
action, the more deeply satisfied I will be.

Second, no matter which way of life I have chosen—
no matter whether it was a well-discerned choice or not—I
am presented each day with myriad choices about how to
live my life, some of them trivial and others more substantial, even momentous: "Should I ask my boss for a raise?"
"Shall I tell the children about my diagnosis of cancer?"
"Shall we have meat loaf for dinner?" "Should I say something to John about his drinking?" "Should I talk to Helen
about how angry she made me last night?" "Shall I accept
the new job I've been offered?" "How shall I vote in today's
election?" These and many other choices confront us daily.
Once again, in responding to the more substantial ones, we
can be more or less in tune with the one action of God.
To become discerning, we need practice in prayerful attention to the movements of our hearts, prayerful reflection
on them, and honest appraisal of what seems more in tune
with God's one action. What leads to greater faith, hope,
and love in our hearts? What seems more likely to enhance
real communion and community among those with whom
we live and work? Conversely, which alternative seems to
close us in on ourselves and make us more fearful and self-
protective? A daily examination of consciousness, like the
one I mentioned at the end of chapter 3, gradually makes us

more finely tuned in to what choices are most in line with God's kingdom. We become more discerning of where the kingdom is present.

Finally, we live in a world of social, political, economic, cultural, and religious institutions that are human creations and that condition our lives and our choices. For example, fifty years ago a Roman Catholic culture dominated the lives of most Catholics to such an extent that they never seriously questioned that deliberately eating meat on Friday merited eternal damnation. Another example: luxuries of twenty years ago are necessities today: "I need my word processor to write this book," "I couldn't live in a place without running hot water," "We have to watch the evening news on television," and "No one can get along without a Blackberry." Moreover, cultural stereotypes condition how we react to people of different races or ethnic origins. These examples illustrate how social and cultural institutions and customs that are human creations condition us.

As human creations these institutions and customs are not automatically in tune with God's one action, which is the kingdom. As Christians, we are called to discern in this area as well as in our personal and interpersonal lives. What structures in our church and our churches, for example, militate against God's intention of a universal community of brothers and sisters? A clear example is racial or ethnic exclusivity. Segregated churches are obviously not where the kingdom of God is present. But we might ask whether the structures that systematically exclude women from the ministry of the word and from the altar (for example, the prohibition of women deacons, priests, and even altar girls) are in tune with the intention of God.

In the social and political realm we must discern whether the institutions human beings have created are in tune with God's one action. The bishops of the United States, for example, asked precisely that question with regard to the nuclear arms policy (in May 1983) and to economic structures and policies (in January 1987) of the United States. Christians need to ask such questions about the health-care system of their country and about its foreign policy, among other things. At the local level the basic ecclesial communities of South America ask such questions about the social, economic, and political structures and policies that impinge on people's lives and make it less or more possible for them to live as brothers and sisters in the Lord.

In these and many other instances discernment is very difficult and fraught with the potential for conflict. It requires much prayer, reading, reflection, and dialogue among the people of God and among all people of goodwill. We do have instances in which the process has worked and institutions more amenable to the values of the kingdom have been created. One recent example occurred in South Africa, where the Truth and Reconciliation Commission chaired by Archbishop Desmond Tutu helped that strife-torn country to a relatively peaceful transition from apart-heid to a multiracial democracy, as detailed in Tutu's book *No Future without Forgiveness.*

The Example of Jesus

Jesus was the human being most perfectly in tune with the one action of God, and so in him preeminently and uniquely the kingdom of God was and is present. But the "not yet" was also in evidence, because he could not persuade even his closest followers that being in tune with the one action of God was for their good no matter what the consequences. Their fears and prejudices got in the way. Earlier we noted with Kenneth Leech that the kingdom of God is not an evolving movement. Because we cannot honestly say that in our age a greater percentage of people are in tune with God's one action than in Jesus' age, that truth is hardly in jeopardy. Even the holiest among us, and perhaps the holiest most of all, are aware of how far they are from being wholly in tune with God's one action. A short examination of conscience and a look at the newspapers or at the evening news will let any of us know how far we are, as individuals and communities, from being in tune with God's one action. The extent to which we fall short is so staggering as to plunge us into despair. Indeed, I wonder whether the bread and circuses of our time—for example, the inanity of much of our entertainment; our conspicuous consumption; and the abuse of alcohol, drugs, and sex—are not ways to stave off the honest look that might lead to despair.

But Jesus looked reality in the eye if any human ever did, and he did not despair. He must have caught glimpses of the kingdom of God, of the power of love to overcome fear and hatred, and he put his faith in that power. He knew that the powers of darkness would try to quench the light, but he trusted that they would not prevail. They might seem to prevail, but God's light (action) would not be quenched. In a trenchant sentence in *Persons in Relation*, John Macmurray says, "The maxim of illusory religion runs: 'Fear not; trust in God and He will see that none of the things you fear will happen to you'; that of real religion, on the contrary, is 'Fear not; the things that you are afraid of are quite likely to happen to you, but they are nothing to be afraid of'" (1991, 171).

Jesus was assailed by all the powers of evil. Like any human being he feared suffering and death. He wanted his Jewish brothers and sisters to believe in and trust Yahweh as Abba, so he did not relish their rejection. He wanted Judas as a friend and companion and must have recoiled at the kiss of betrayal. But he trusted in Abba to see him through, so these evils ultimately were nothing to be afraid of. We, too, can beg Jesus to help us trust in God and show us how to grow more and more attuned to the kingdom of God, more discerning of the presence of that kingdom in our world. At the same time, may he help us to recognize that every such discernment is still only a glimpse, a foretaste of the reign that is the culmination of God's intention to unite all things in Jesus.

As you ponder this meditation, does it ring true to you? Where do you have questions and objections? Such questions and objections may provide you some food for thought for your ongoing conversation with God and with your friends.

6

Union with God or Finding God's Will?

In the previous two chapters we reflected on discernment and the kingdom of God and on God's intention in creating the world. The question of our role in God's project in creation raises a question that has caused disagreement among spiritual writers in the past. God's love, we argued, is not utilitarian. God just loves us and wants our friendship. That love is not conditioned on whether or not we get with the program. This argument would lead to the conclusion that spiritual practices should aim toward union or friendship with God. But throughout Christian history spiritual practices have aimed to find the will of God, which makes it seem as though God's love is indeed utilitarian. God has a will and wants us to discover it. In this meditation I want to offer a solution to this disagreement that will point toward the kind of healthy living spiritual practices envisage.

The argument about the purpose of spiritual practices shows itself among Jesuit authors who disagree about the purpose of the Spiritual Exercises. Is the purpose union with God or making a decision about how to live one's life (finding God's will)? Finding God's will often has seemed to be a quest to discover what God wants me to do or has created me to do; then we are not far from developing an image of God as the Master Planner who wants people to fit into the overall plan. This image makes God seem rather impersonal. If the purpose of the spiritual life is to attain union with God, then we are not far from developing an image of God as lover who wants to hold us in embrace. This image worries people who believe that God wants us to try to make the world a better place. Both images have a long history, and both can be defended as orthodox, but both leave something to be desired as far as full Christian practice is concerned. Is there a way to understand the Christian spiritual life that will unite these two seemingly competing theories?

God's One Action

Often enough the search for the will of God presupposes a divine blueprint that exists from all eternity and leaves God strangely outside the action involved in carrying out the blueprint. The blueprint is eternal; our task is to figure out our part in the plan with the help of the Holy Spirit. But we often do not advert to God's ongoing activity in creation when we try to figure out our part in the blueprint. To begin my response to the question, "Union with God or finding God's will?" I want to offer a way to envision creation not as an action that took place once in the distant past, but as God's ongoing action.

As I wrote in the previous chapter, we can follow the thought of John Macmurray and think of the universe as one divine action governed by one intention. To get some idea of what I mean, try thinking of some large and comprehensive decision you made, say, to get married, to create a work of art, or to teach a course on auto mechanics. Each of these decisions can be seen as leading to a very complex and multifaceted single action. In the previous chapter I referred to the action of writing and publishing this book to get across a sense of what I mean by one action. This one action of publishing a book is governed by my intention of writing a book that will help people with their prayer, and it includes many other actions and events that occur over a relatively long time. The action ends when the book is published and others read it, because my intention in writing the book is to have an effect on readers. You might want to work out some of the components of the comprehensive action you undertook. You will realize how complex and lengthy in time this one action is. Now let's use the analogy of our one action and apply it to God's one action that creates and sustains our universe.

Think of this vast, mysterious universe as one action of God. This one action includes all the events that have occurred and ever will occur in its existence: the evolution of the galaxies; the countless collisions of matter; the development of planetary systems, including our own; and finally our own planet revolving around our sun, thus enabling the earth to evolve plant, animal, and human life. Consider this whole complex universe as one action of God. If God were to stop acting, the universe would cease to exist. This one action exists because God wants it to exist and only because God wants it to exist. The universe's existence depends, at every moment of its existence, on the gossamer thread, as it were, of God's desire.

With the advent of beings with intellect and will (personal beings) God's one creative action includes the actions of all these personal beings who have existed or ever will exist. Their actions, like God's one action, are governed by purpose or intention. Hence, God's one action includes all the purposeful actions that have ever existed or will exist within this one action, whether these actions are in tune with God's intention or not. When we think of creation along these lines, the complexity and enormity of what God's action entails staggers our minds. We can never grasp the mystery of this creation.

God's Intention in Creating

Why does God create this universe? Like any personal action, God's creative activity has a purpose or intention. But, as noted in the previous chapter, we can know the intention of anyone only if that person chooses to reveal it. I may infer your intention or purpose, but I can be sure of what you intend only if you communicate your intention to me. We can know God's intention in creating the universe only if God chooses to reveal it to us. We believe that God has most clearly revealed God's purpose through interaction with a particular people, the people of Israel, and finally and definitively in one member of that people, Jesus of Nazareth. We believe that the Bible is a record of God's interaction and self-communication and that through reflection on the Bible we can know God's purpose or intention in creating our world. What is that intention?

I have come to believe that God, in creating our planet at any rate, wants the friendship and cooperation of all human beings. In other words, God creates this universe, in which human beings evolve, for the sake of our friendship and co-operation. This thesis seems humanly egocentric, but we have to remember what we believe, namely, that God actually became a human being and lived and died "for us and for our salvation," as we say in our creed. In John's Gospel we read, "God so loved the world that he gave his only Son, so that everyone who believes in him may not perish but may have eternal life" (John 3:16); and later, "And this is eternal life, that they may know you, the only true God, and Jesus Christ whom you have sent" (John 17:3). The verb *know* in the preceding sentence refers to heart knowledge, the kind of knowing that friends experience with one another. Our belief in the incarnation entails belief in some sort of special relationship between God and human beings. It may seem egocentric for us human beings to come to this conclusion, but it seems the clear sense of God's revelation. Are you with me so far?

If creation is one action of God governed by one intention, then God is always active in creation, not only sustaining the one action that is creation but also sustaining it purposefully. That is, God is always working to bring about God's intention in this one action that is the world. If, therefore, God creates our world to call all human beings to friendship with God, then God is always actively pursuing this purpose. With this realization we are in a position to rethink the meaning of union with God in a way that includes finding God's will.

Union with God Means Finding God's Will

God invites us human beings into friendship. But friendship and cooperation cannot be coerced. God cannot have what God wants without our consent, without our free engagement in that friendship. In creating this universe God becomes that vulnerable. The divine purpose depends on human cooperation and friendship. A haunting line in Denise Levertov's poem "Annunciation" brings home this vulnerability: "God waited (*The Stream and the Sapphire*, 1997, 59)." God waited for Mary's acceptance of the offer, just as God waits on our acceptance.

However, God actively works in this world to draw us into such friendship and cooperation. We Christians attribute this activity to the Holy Spirit, who moves our hearts and minds to accept the offer. Union, therefore, is union with God actively trying to draw all human beings into a harmonious community with God, with one another, and with the whole created cosmos, which is the environment in which all of us exist.

With this line of reasoning union does not mean resting in the embrace of an inactive God. Rather, it seems to be an invitation to joint activity with God in achieving God's one intention in creating the universe. We are being invited to a friendship with God that helps God to fulfill God's desire. Just as with Mary, God waits on our response. God cannot achieve the dream without our free acceptance of the offer of friendship and cooperation.

In the first chapter of Genesis we read that human beings are created in God's own image and likeness and are given dominion over the animals and plants on the earth. In spite of the misuse of this text to justify the destruction of the environment for humanity's sake, one can read it as in invitation to friendship and cooperation with God's project for the universe. One can think of this invitation as analogous to a parent's invitation to children to join the family business. God invites us to join God's family business, which is the cultivation of this universe in harmony with one another and with the environment around us.

A Spiritual Practice

Given this argument, we can begin to see how union with God entails action on our part. If we are created for friendship and cooperation with God in the family business that is the universe, then our deepest happiness will consist in accepting the invitation, that is, in engaging in a relationship of friendship and cooperation with God active in this world. Such an engagement entails accepting a spiritual practice. One cannot become a friend of anyone without engaging in the disciplined and demanding practice of mutual communication and cooperation. This is even truer of becoming a friend of God. If we accept the invitation, we will be engaging in a demanding discipline. Before all of you stop reading, let me assure you that this discipline does not demand spending hours in prayer on your knees. We need to take seriously the analogy of human friendship here. The discipline required is not much different from what is required in a human friendship. Of course, we need to spend time with people if we are going to become friends, but it need not take up the whole of our life. Let me point to some of the elements needed for the development of a friendship with God.

To develop friendship with God we need to notice that we desire such a friendship. We become friends of others because we want to. I believe that God, in desiring us into existence for friendship, creates in us a correlative desire for friendship with God. Those who pay attention to this desire will want to grow in closeness and friendship with God. This will require spending time with God to develop the friendship. If you want some pointers on ways to engage in such prayer, you can see my book *A Friendship Like No Other.* Briefly, it means spending time talking to God and listening to what God wants to communicate with you. It's as simple as that. It does not require long hours each day, just some time to be in God's presence. Such time could be as little as a few minutes reflecting on the day, noticing when we felt most alive and whole, a sign that we were experiencing God's presence. If people engage in the discipline of trying to become aware of God's presence, they will become aware of such times. They will also become aware of times when they are far from experiencing God's presence, times when they are out of tune with the kind of friendship God wants with us. When they notice such differences, they are beginning the process called the discernment of spirits. Here is where the question that began this chapter receives its final answer.

Attuning Our Hearts

If God is actively working to draw all human beings into friendship and cooperation in God's family business, then we can understand the ancient discipline of the discernment of spirits as our way of letting God do that work of attraction in our hearts. For our hearts are not automatically in tune with God's desire in creation; they are drawn toward many actions that lead us away from friendship with God. Our hearts need to become attuned to the one action of God drawing all human beings into friendship. God's Spirit dwelling in our hearts can become the tuning fork that enables our hearts to be attuned to God's action, but we need to engage in disciplined reflection to notice the Spirit's promptings. Such disciplined reflection begins when we notice the difference between those times when we feel most alive and whole and those times when we seem caught up in fear and self-absorption. The first seem to be movements in tune with what God wants in creation; the second seem to run counter to what God wants.

Darrell Jones, a prisoner I visit who has become a friend, provides an example of such discernment. I knew from previous conversations that Darrell had had a conversion experience in prison. At one visit I asked him what had precipitated the change in him, expecting to hear of some prayer experience. What he said was stunning in its simplicity and honesty. "I began to care for a woman who was visiting me. Once I began to care for her, I realized that I couldn't keep on living as I had been living." All it took was paying attention to the movement toward friendship with another human being and acting on that movement.

I hesitate to use the language of finding God's will at this point of a discussion of discernment because it can so easily lead to the image of God as the Master Planner. I prefer to see the discernment of spirits as a way to attune our hearts to the intention of God in creation. That intention, as I have argued, is that we all be drawn into friendship with God. If we are trying to attune our hearts with this intention, then we will gradually grow more like God; that is, we will gradually become more like the images of God we are created to be. In that sense we will find the will of God. That's what Darrell was doing, I believe.

This process of becoming more like God will require facing up to our failures to live as images of God in the past and repenting those failures. God does have standards, after all, and as we grow in friendship with God, we realize that we have failed to live up to those standards and will continue to fail if we are not helped by the grace of God. In this process of facing up to our failures, both our personal failures and our communal failures, we will come to realize the truth of the words in John's Gospel cited earlier, "God so loved the world that he gave his only Son, so that everyone who believes in him may not perish but may have eternal life" (John 3:16). We recognize that if we were to continue on the path of our sinful failures we would perish. But we also recognize that Jesus, God's only Son, died for our sins and for the sins of the whole world and, thus, made it possible for all of us to repent and move back into the path of friendship with God. Moreover, we also realize that God has not given up on our world, but is still working to bring about the divine intention in creating it. The realization of God's continued and continual action in the world lifts a tremendous weight from our hearts and minds; we feel free and whole, and we want to become part of the solution to the world's problems insofar as we can.

A New Turn

A new turn in the growth in our friendship with God can now take place. In the Wisdom of Solomon we read of Wisdom: "in every generation she passes into holy souls / and makes them friends of God, and prophets" (Wisdom

7:27). For Christians who have grown this far in friendship through contemplation of Jesus dying on the cross for us and for our salvation, the Spirit (Wisdom) rouses the desire to become a friend of Jesus. To become his friend means to grow into his image and likeness, to become his disciple. Friends of Jesus want to live in this world in tune with the values and dreams of Jesus, to become part of God's family business in earnest. Jesus was about his Father's business in his life. To become a disciple of Jesus means to be about the Father's business. This does not require becoming a religious professional. It means living in whatever way of life as a friend of God in the image and likeness of Jesus, sharing his values and priorities. Darrell is trying to do this to the best of his ability in prison.

I grow in friendship with Jesus by contemplating the stories of his life portrayed in the Gospels with the desire to know him better in order to love and follow him more faithfully. In the course of growing in knowledge and love of him, I will have to continue to notice and discern the different movements of my heart and mind. The discernment of spirits, then, requires that I pay attention to what friendship with Jesus entails. It means overcoming my fears of openness and honesty in my relationship with Jesus. So I grow in my willingness to share what is in my heart with him and to listen to what he has to say to me. In the process I begin to see that certain ways of acting and responding to life are not compatible with being Jesus' friend, just as Darrell noticed that his previous way of living was not compatible with caring for the woman who visited him. I notice that Jesus forgives those who fail and offend him and realize that I, too, am called to forgive those who fail and offend me. I see that he has a predilection for those who are poor and marginalized, and I feel the tug to follow him in this predilection. I see him forgive enemies like Saul of Tarsus, and I desire to become like him. In other words, the discernment of spirits comes naturally as I grow in my knowledge and love of Jesus; I just want to be like him, and I notice when my reactions are like his and when they are not. I am attuning my heart to his way of being a human being and thus becoming more like the human being I am created to be, an image of God. In this process, of course, I become part of a community of disciples that, in principle, wants to include all human beings.

Everyday Decisions Have Large Implications

You will notice that this account of the discernment of spirits focuses not on large decisions, but on everyday reactions and behavior. Of course, I may want to use the techniques of discernment to make large decisions, such as to decide on my vocation in life, but such use comes only after I have developed the habit of discernment through the discipline of developing the friendship that God wants with me and with every human being. With such discernment we attune more of our everyday actions to God's intention in creating the world; that is, we grow in friendship with Jesus and seek to engage in friendly cooperation with others. We try to bring about conditions more in keeping with God's dream of a universal community of human beings living in harmony with one another and with the whole of creation. These actions of ours may not be momentous, but they do make a difference in the little part of the world for which we have some responsibility. I prefer this language of attunement to that of finding God's will because the latter can tend to put all the emphasis on the big decisions, such as finding one's calling in life, and to neglect the daily discernment needed to cooperate in God's family business.

If we do grow in friendship with Jesus in this way, we will be doing God's will. We will have accepted the invitation to friendship that God intends in creating us and we will be engaged in cooperating in God's family business, which is creating a world in which all human beings are friends of God and of one another and are living harmoniously with all of creation. Thus, union with God and finding God's will come together in the process of developing friendship with God. Discerning God's will means attuning ourselves with God's intention in creation and thus entails union with God. While engaging in the process of growing in friendship with God, we will also be growing into the kind of mature human beings we were created to be, men and women who can, in the words of Sigmund Freud, love and work, care for others for their sakes and work productively in this world. Thus, spiritual practice can lead to psychological maturity.

I end with this insightful paragraph from a talk by Peter-Hans Kolvenbach to the members of the Society of Jesus' Thirty-fourth General Congregation: "Ignatius proclaims that for human beings there is no authentic search for God without an insertion into the life of the creation, and that, on the other hand, all solidarity with human beings and every engagement with the created world cannot be authentic without a discovery of God" (1995, 53).

7

Decision Making in the Ignatian Tradition

We have been discussing discernment from various points of view. In this meditation I want to use some concrete examples to illustrate Ignatian decision making. The first examples come from the life of Ignatius of Loyola himself. The second is a hypothetical case of a young man making a decision about a way of life. I hope that reflection on these examples will help you to get into a habit of making decisions in the light of your own experience of God's movements in your heart.

Ignatius's Election as General Superior

In 1539 Ignatius was strangely reluctant to take on the role of general superior of the new Society of Jesus when his

companions elected him. He first refused the office, protesting that he was too great a sinner, preferred to obey than to
command, and was unable to govern himself. He begged
the companions to reconsider the matter for four more days.
When they again voted the same way, Ignatius went to his
confessor and engaged in three days of careful review of his
past life and made a general confession. He asked the confessor to make the decision as to whether he should take the
office. When the confessor told him that a refusal would
be resistance to the will of God, Ignatius remained uncon-
vinced and asked the confessor to pray over the matter for
three more days and then submit his decision in writing.
Finally, when the confessor's decision remained the same,
he gave in and accepted the office. His repeated hesitation,
given his clear leadership role in the small group, strikes the
modern reader as odd if not disingenuous.

The Jesuit psychoanalyst William Meissner, having
gone over these details, attributes Ignatius's hesitations to
his ambivalence and to the residues of ambition and nar-
cissism that Ignatius abhorred in himself (*Ignatius of Loyola*,
1992, 181–84). It is also possible that he feared that some
of the escapades of his earlier life would become known
and would be used to harm the new congregation. He had
also, it seems, offended a then influential cardinal, Vincent
Carafa, founder of the Theatines and future Pope Paul IV, by
a rather harsh critique of the ways of that new congregation.

Whatever triggered his initial reluctance, once he accepted the task, he showed no hesitation about the use of his authority, even to the point of severely reprimanding the very companions whom he always considered cofounders of the nascent Society of Jesus.

Let's reflect for a moment on this sequence of events in the life of Ignatius. Something in Ignatius's spirit did not feel totally at ease with his election. This was a decisive moment, not only for his life, but also for this new enterprise, the Society of Jesus. Ignatius wanted to be sure that his election was in tune with God's will. I believe that this uncertainty, wherever it came from, lay behind his subsequent actions. No matter whether his reluctance came from psychological sources, from fears of scandal, or from a deeply spiritual sense that his calling was not to administration, his uncertainty was a reality that he felt he had to take seriously.

To be sure, he and the companions needed to storm heaven to ask for more light. When this procedure produced the same result, Ignatius still felt unsure. So he spoke with his confessor at some length. He needed to be sure not just for his own sake but also for the sake of the Society of Jesus, which he and his first companions believed God wanted to exist. Ignatius prayed earnestly because it was important to get it right.

I believe that we have, in this story, the keys to a spirituality of decision making in the Ignatian tradition. For Ignatius and the first companions the decision about who should lead the new Society of Jesus was very important. They believed that God wanted the Society to exist and to prosper. Now that Pope Paul III had approved the Society, the companions needed to elect a general superior who would not only lead the fledging group but also draft its constitutions. This election, therefore, would be crucial for the solid foundation and hoped-for progress of the Society. Consequently, Ignatius and his companions prayed to God for guidance to make the right choice. They took it for granted that God had a stake in the decision they were about to make and would give them guidance in their deliberations.

Second, they listened for the divine response, and that response, it seems, could come through many avenues: the votes of the companions, the advice of Ignatius's confessor, and their own interior movements to which they paid attention before and after their votes. Ignatius and his companions presumed that God has a dream that includes not only what individuals do but also what a group does, and that God would communicate that dream to them. Included among the ways they expected God to communicate were not only their own individual discernment of what the Spirit was communicating to each of them but also the misgivings of one of them, namely, Ignatius. Included, too, was the advice of Ignatius's confessor, who also had to face in his own prayer the force of Ignatius's reluctance to take on the job. God's will, in other words, is made known in the messiness of the real world.

Once Ignatius had done all that he could do to resolve his hesitations and had concluded that he should accept the job, he never looked back or worried about whether he had done the right thing. In this chapter I want to continue our reflection on discernment and to spell out some of the implications of this example of Ignatian decision making for our own decision making.

What Kinds of Decisions?

What kinds of decisions are we talking about? Clearly the decision facing the first Jesuits was rather momentous. It had implications not only for the men themselves but also for the church. At least with hindsight we can say this because, in its more than 450 years of existence, the Society of Jesus has had such a strong influence on the church. But momentous, too, are many of the decisions we make in life. The choice to get married, and to a particular person, has implications not only for the two people involved but also for their families of origin and for the future generations who will, perhaps, trace their origins to this couple with unknown consequences for the world. Clearly it is a momentous choice. Hence, couples contemplating marriage want to be sure that they are making the right choice. The decision to join a religious congregation also has consequences, not only because there will be no future family but also because the entrant will affect the congregation for good or ill and touch an untold number of lives, again with unknown consequences for the world and the church. Anyone making this choice wants to be sure about the decision. In fact, if one thinks about it a bit, many of the decisions we make have consequences with effects on the history of the world.

I have been a Jesuit for more than fifty-five years. In those years I have had an impact on the Society of Jesus and on many people, some of whom have met me only through my writing. If I had not decided to enter the College of the Holy Cross in 1948, I might never have thought to become a Jesuit. The decision to go to Holy Cross was momentous in my life. Yet I went there almost by accident, without much thought at all. Many can say the same thing about their own choices of where to go for an education. All of our choices have consequences, some of them more significant than others.

God's Stake in Our Choices

Does God have a stake in our choices? Ignatius obviously believed that God did. The whole purpose of the Spiritual Exercises is to help people make choices that are more in accord with God's dream and not driven by inordinate attachments. How are we to understand God's role in our choices?

As we saw in the previous chapter, we can understand the world as the one ongoing action of God. God is always active in this world working out the divine intention, the kingdom of God, where all people live in harmonious unity with the triune God, with one another, and with the whole created universe. God's one action that is this world includes all the actions of human beings and all the things that happen without human intention. Our actions can be more or less in tune with God's one purposeful action. Hence, we can say that God has a stake in all our choices.

In the "Contemplation to Obtain Love" of the Spiritual Exercises, Ignatius has the exercitant ask for the grace to experience "how God dwells in creatures; . . . and finally, how in this way he dwells also in myself, giving me existence, life, sensation, and intelligence; and even further, making me his temple, since I am created as a likeness and image of the Divine Majesty" (#235) and "how God labors and works for me in all the creatures on the face of the earth" (#236). Ignatius believes that people can experience, in faith, God acting purposefully in our world. When they do have this experience, they are then faced with the question of whether, first, they want to and, then, how they can align their own lives and actions with the divine action. In principle, every conscious action can be more or less in tune with God's one action that is the world. When we look at our actions in this light, then all of them somehow seem momentous because they can either be aligned with God's action or be out of tune with that action. In some real way every time we choose a course of action, we cooperate with

God's one action, or we fail to cooperate. On this understanding God has a stake in all our choices.

The question is whether we will take God's interest seriously enough to try to discern how our choices fit in with God's dream for the world. Given Ignatius's own experiences and conviction of the divine indwelling and activity in the world, it is no wonder that he wanted to be sure that his decisions and his election as general superior were in tune with God's desire. If we were so convinced, would we not want to be sure?

The Complexity of Discernment of Any Action

Ignatian decision making rests on the assumption that God has a purpose in creating the world and each of us. Often enough we speak of finding the will of God. As I wrote in the previous chapter, this can sound like trying to discover an eternal plan that God has willed for each of us. The reality can, however, be a more complicated affair than it first appears to be. For example, it seems that Ignatius discerned at Manresa that God wanted him to spend his life in the Holy Land helping souls. Events proved Ignatius wrong in this discernment, at least as far as living and dying in Jerusalem is concerned. He was ordered to leave the Holy Land by the Franciscan provincial superior, who threatened Ignatius with excommunication if he disobeyed. Ignatius concluded that it was not God's will for him to remain there. Thus, determining the will of God can be complicated; it is not just a case of our subjective personal discernment.

Ignatius provides another example. In 1552 Emperor Charles V presented the name of Francis Borja, the former duke of Gandía, now a Jesuit priest, to Pope Julius III to be given the cardinal's hat, and the pope was disposed to do it. Ignatius wrote to Borja an account of his own experience and his process of discernment as to what he (Ignatius) should do in this regard. After three days of some emotional turmoil and prayer Ignatius came to the conclusion that he should do all in his power to stop the process. He wrote:

> I felt sure at the time, and still feel so, that, if I did not act thus, I should not be able give a good account of myself to God Our Lord—indeed, that I should give quite a bad one.
>
> Therefore, I have felt, and now feel, that it is God's will that I oppose this move. Even though others might think otherwise, and bestow this dignity on you, I do not see that there would be any contradiction, since the same Spirit could move me to this action for certain reasons and others to the contrary for other reasons, and thus bring about the result desired by the emperor. May God our Lord always do what will be to His greater praise and glory. (Young, *Letters*, 1959, 258)

Finding the will of God in the real world is not a simple matter of one's own personal discernment. Other actors and factors come into play.

Ignatius presumed that God might inspire people to different conclusions regarding the same issue. I prefer to say that God works with all decisions, even those that may not be in tune with God's dream. I like the Portuguese proverb quoted by Paul Claudel as the epigraph of his play *The Satin Slipper*, "God writes straight with crooked lines." All our actions, even the best intentioned and most finely discerned, are crooked lines, flawed and human; yet God works with them all to bring about the kingdom.

As a result of such considerations I prefer to use the phrase "the will of God" in this sense: God is working at all times in this world to bring about God's intention or project, the kingdom of God, if you will. Human beings are called to attune themselves to this work of God, to God's project. The discernment of spirits revolves around this belief that God is acting at all times and that we can be more or less in tune with the divine action or out of tune. So when we discern, we are not searching for the eternal plan God decreed for each one of us. Rather, we are trying to align our actions, to the best of our abilities, with the one divine action that is the world. We do all in our power to attune our actions with God's action, but then we have to leave the rest to God and to the interplay of the actions and events outside our control.

How Do We Attune Our Actions with God's One Action?

This leads to the question of how we attune our actions with the one action of God. Again, Ignatius and the first companions show us a way. We have already seen how they acted when they came to the question of the election of the first general superior of the Society. When we are faced with a decision, we need to bring God into the picture and use all the rules of discernment to become aware of the movements of our hearts when we ask God for enlightenment. But we also may need to ask others for help in our discernment and pay attention to their advice and recommendations. In other words, we do the best we can to discern how our projected action aligns itself with God's dream for us and for the world. Like Ignatius, we want to be sure that we are as closely in tune with God's action as we can be. Once we have done our best to discern, we try to put our decision into action in a complicated world where we are not the only actors.

Let me give an example. Suppose a young man is trying to discern whether he has a vocation to religious life, and specifically to the Society of Jesus. He needs to do some homework to find out something about the Jesuit order, its spirituality, its ethos, and its work. If he finds that there is a positive resonance with his own dreams and hopes, he begs God for light to discern whether God wants him to make application. He believes that God has a stake in his decision. How he decides to live his life will have repercussions not only for his own life but also for all those with whom he will come in contact once he has decided on a way of life. He wants to be sure, just as Ignatius wanted to be sure, that he will be in tune with God's dream for the world. In his process of discernment he speaks with a spiritual director who helps him to pay attention to all that is going on his heart and mind. He talks with friends who know him and who know the Jesuits.

Let's suppose that he comes to the firm decision that God is calling him to join the Society of Jesus. Now he must make an application and follow all the procedures required of applicants. It is not a foregone conclusion that he will be accepted. He has no control of the decision of the Society. He must now leave that in the hands of the Jesuits and of God.

There is a saying often attributed to Ignatius that goes like this: "Pray as if everything depended on God; work as if everything depended on you." Ignatius never wrote or said anything like this, but a Swiss Jesuit, some years after Ignatius's death, created some pithy Latin sayings, called "little sparks," attributed to Ignatius. These were based on things Ignatius wrote and said and on his spirituality, but they were not direct quotations. A rough translation of one of them runs: "Let this be the first rule of action: trust in God as though the success of the venture depended solely on you, not on God; at the same time give yourself to the work as though God alone were to do everything." In other words, the saying seems to mean exactly the opposite of the usual one attributed to Ignatius. It should run: "pray as if everything depended on you; work as if everything depended on God." With this little spark, I believe, we are at the heart of decision making in the Ignatian tradition.

Before I make a significant decision, I need to pray as if everything depended on me in the following sense: What I decide has some place in God's dream for the world because God is always at work to bring about that dream. God will work with my decision whether it is in tune or out of tune with the divine dream. But it makes a difference whether or not my action is in tune. Think of the choice Mary of Nazareth faced. God waited, as it were, on her response to Gabriel's announcement. She could have refused, and then, we presume, God would have worked with that choice to bring about what God wants to do. But the world would have taken a different course. The Son of God would not have been the Jesus of Nazareth we now know. Mary's was, no doubt, one of the most momentous choices ever made in our world. But its singular significance should not blind us to the fact that all of our choices, at least the more-than-ordinary ones, have some effect on the world that is God's one action. Hence, God has a stake in these choices and, in some mysterious way, depends on us. So I pray as if everything depended on me.

Once I have discerned, to the best of my ability, what action is more in tune with God's action, then I act as if everything depended on God. That is, I must leave the success or failure of what I do up to God and to the other actors in our world and to events. This is what Jesus had to do once he discerned that his vocation called for him to go to Jerusalem and make the final attempt to call his people to repentance and to belief in him. He went to his death trusting that God would bring about God's dream through this horror. So too, we followers of Jesus do the best we can to align our actions with that dream and then leave resurrection to the Father.

If the young man who has applied to the Jesuits is living out of this tradition, he will be able to recover his equilibrium if he is not accepted, just as Ignatius recovered his equilibrium when the Franciscan provincial ordered him to leave the Holy Land. It may not be easy, but the point is that he is trying to attune his actions with the one action of God. If he is rejected, he now needs to move on with his life, continuing to try to discover how his life can best be attuned with God's action. It may even be that the Jesuits have made a mistake in rejecting him. That's not the point. In the real world we can only do our best to discern God's will and then leave the rest to God, trusting that God will write straight with whatever crooked lines we and others write.

How do these thoughts about discernment strike you? Do they make sense? Enough sense to want to try to become more attuned with God's dream for our world?

PART III

On Present Dilemmas

✧

In this part I offer meditations on some of the dilemmas modern Christians face in living in friendship with God and in tune with God's dream for our world. We are living in a time of momentous change and can often feel afraid and anxious. These meditations address some of the fears evoked in us and aim to help readers engage more deeply in a relationship of friendship with God.

✧

8

What Is the Real World?

Religious people who try to live in accordance with their religious beliefs—for example, with the kind of belief about God's dream and our part in it of the previous few chapters—will sometimes encounter comments like this: "Get with the real world. You can't live with your head in the clouds. In the real world you have to leave your religion for Sundays." We can feel threatened by such comments, left wondering if the others are right. After all we, too, like our irreligious neighbors, live in what seems a rather dark and dismal time. I want to ponder with you the question, "What is the real world?"

Two Opposing Views of the Real World

Let's start with two poems written by Englishmen in the late nineteenth century, which give diametrically opposite answers to this question. The first is Matthew Arnold's poem "Dover Beach" written in 1867:

> The sea is calm tonight.
> The tide is full, the moon lies fair
> Upon the straits; on the French coast the light
> Gleams and is gone; the cliffs of England stand,
> Glimmering and vast, out in the tranquil bay.
> Come to the window, sweet is the night-air!
> Only, for the long line of spray
> Where the sea meets the moon-blanched land,
> Listen! You hear the grating roar
> Of pebbles which the waves draw back, and fling,
> At their return, up the high strand,
> Begin, and cease, and then again begin,
> With tremulous cadence slow, and bring
> The eternal note of sadness in.
>
> Sophocles long ago
> Heard it on the Aegean, and it brought
> Into his mind the turbid ebb and flow
> Of human misery; we

Find also in the sound a thought,
Hearing it by this distant northern sea.

The sea of Faith
Was once, too, at the full, and round earth's shore
Lay like the folds of a bright girdle furled.
But now I only hear
Its melancholy, long, withdrawing roar,
Retreating, to the breath
Of the night-wind, down the vast edges drear
And naked shingles of the world.

Ah, love, let us be true
To one another! For the world, which seems
To lie before us like a land of dreams,
So various, so beautiful, so new,
Hath really neither joy, nor love, nor light,
Nor certitude, nor peace, nor help for pain;
And we are here as on a darkling plain
Swept with confused alarms of struggle and flight,
Where ignorant armies clash by night.

Many of us might find this 150-year-old poem speaking to us in this new century where ignorant armies clash by night and by day, and where, we fear, the sea of faith retreats down the drear edges of our shores. Does Arnold describe the real world?

Or is the real world the one that Gerard Manley Hopkins describes in "God's Grandeur," written ten years after "Dover Beach" in 1877?

> The world is charged with the grandeur of God.
> It will flame out, like shining from shook foil;
> It gathers to a greatness, like the ooze of oil
> Crushed. Why do men then now not reck his rod?
> Generations have trod, have trod, have trod;
> And all is seared with trade; bleared, smeared with
>   toil;
> And wears man's smudge and shares man's smell: the
>   soil
> Is bare now, nor can foot feel, being shod.
>   And, for all this, nature is never spent;
>   There lives the dearest freshness deep down
>   things;
>   And though the last lights off the black West went
>   Oh, morning, at the brown brink eastwards,
>   springs–
>   Because the Holy Ghost over the bent
>   World broods with warm breast and with ah!
>   bright Wings.

Such a vision cheers many of us, but is it a pipe dream given the reality that goes on all around us? Which poem speaks of the real world?

Both of these poets lived at the same time in Victorian England, when Great Britain bestrode the world as a colossus and seemed to be at the height of its imperial grandeur. But the imperial grandeur did not preclude wars and rumors of wars, enormous disparities between the wealthy and the poor, early death by disease, and the pollution caused by the Industrial Revolution. Clearly both poets felt the dark side of things in their age, and both, it seems, were prone to dark moods. Hopkins, we know, often felt despair. Among other things, he never saw a single poem of his published. Yet "God's Grandeur" attests that he was able to overcome his tendency to depression and despair. But the question remains, "Which poet is describing the real world?" I want to discuss this issue because we live in dark times, both in the world and in our church, in this new century and millennium when the United States bestrides the world as a colossus and seems at the height of its grandeur and power.

According to Arnold the real world is a world in which faith no longer helps; the poem drips with sadness at the loss of faith. There is nothing to rely on. The only hope is to cling to those we love. In our new century the vitality and hope that buoyed many people after the

Second World War seems to have been sucked out of us. We can, perhaps, resonate with the sentiments of "Dover Beach." Natural disasters, global warming, wars, and terrorism have knocked any optimism out of us. For citizens of the United States the attack on the World Trade Center and the Pentagon on September 11, 2001, blew away any illusions that our homeland was immune from terrorist attacks. In addition, the aftermath of that attack and the wars in Afghanistan and then in Iraq have left us feeling even more vulnerable and afraid. It's as though we have been hit in the stomach with a powerful body punch; the air has just gone out of us. We live in a world in which fear is rampant.

Moreover, the Roman Catholic Church in many places in the world has been dealt a vicious body blow by the accusations and reality of sexual abuse by many priests and religious; by the precipitous decline in the number of priests and religious, at least in the developed world; and by the need to close large, empty churches in many of our cities. In many parts of the church wide fissures between and among Catholics have sapped energy and caused waves of sadness, if not of depression. We can, indeed, feel the pinch of Arnold's poem. Perhaps he and others who have lost hope are living in the real world while those of us who, like Hopkins, maintain hope live in a world of empty dreams.

The Source of Hopkins's Hope

Remember that Hopkins lived in the same country and at the same time as Matthew Arnold. Remember, too, that Hopkins was not a man of sunny disposition. Yet Hopkins could write with passion, "There lives the dearest freshness deep down things," in spite of all the pain and suffering, in spite of the stupidity and the evil human beings are capable of, and in spite of his own dark moods. What made it possible for him to write these words?

Every year of his Jesuit life Hopkins made the Spiritual Exercises of Ignatius, twice in their full thirty-day form, every other time for eight days. During these days of prayer he asked to see the world through God's eyes in the last great contemplation of the Exercises, the "Contemplation to Attain Love." This contemplation is the culmination of the retreat. The one who makes it asks for "interior knowledge of all the great good I have received, in order that, stirred to profound gratitude, I may become able to love and serve the Divine Majesty in all things." During this contemplation one asks to recall one's creation and salvation and all the particular gifts one has received in life.

"I will ponder," writes Ignatius, "with deep affection how much God our Lord has done for me, and how much God has given me of what God possesses, and consequently how God desires to give me God's own self insofar as God can do so." In addition, I ask to experience how God dwells in everything; how God labors and works for me in everything on the face of the earth; and how all good things and gifts descend from above. In other words, the one making the retreat wants to experience this world as "charged with the grandeur of God." Apparently Hopkins received what he asked for.

The questions each of us face are the ones Hopkins and all human beings face: Is there reason for hope? Do we see glimmers of light in our darkness? Let me say some things about the real world for those who believe in the God of Jewish and Christian Scriptures.

The Real World according to Scripture

The real world, according to our Scriptures, is God's creation, created out of nothing except God's desire for its existence. God wants this world to exist. Moreover, in the very first chapter of Scripture, in the book of Genesis, God is depicted as creating this world with a lavishness, generosity, and bounty that seem to have no bounds except the bounds of the world itself. To the animals, birds, and fish, and to human beings as well, God asks for the same generosity and bounty. We hear God say, "Increase and multiply." This, of course, means procreation, but it can also be understood as urging us to make more of ourselves; to be our best selves; to be like God in creativity, generosity, and love.

In addition, one can read the second story of creation (chapters 2 and 3 of Genesis) as a story of God creating the world as a garden in which human beings cooperate in friendship with God and one another and with the whole of creation. In this story the human beings are naked and are not ashamed, a symbol of their transparency before God and each other. Sin brings in fear and shame, throws a monkey wrench into God's dream. But God does not give up on the dream. God calls Abraham and Sarah to become God's friends and cooperators, a beginning of the reversal of the effects of sin in the world. In other words, God creates us in God's own image to live in friendship with God, with all other human beings, and with the whole of creation, and even human sin has not derailed God's dream.

In this continuing story of God and the world God finally takes up residence in our world in the person of Jesus of Nazareth, who calls people into friendship with him and with one another. "I have called you friends"; "love one another as I have loved you" (John 15:15, 12). We believe that Jesus, the Jew of Galilee, is so one with God that he is God. And he is risen from the dead, bodily risen. The body is different than ours, but it is a body. Bodies have physical ties with the whole universe. So the particles that make up Jesus' body swirl through this universe. Heaven is not out there. In some real way it's right here.

In addition, we believe that the Holy Spirit of God dwells in human hearts. God's Spirit animates our desires, our hopes, our dreams, and moves us to want what God wants. And this Spirit dwells in real people like us. And we are part of the real world. "The world is charged with the grandeur of God; it will flame out like shining from shook foil." This, then, we believe, is the real world. If it's not, then our faith is, indeed, a pipe dream.

If what we Christians believe is true, then the real world is the world described in Hopkins's poem "God's Grandeur," not the one of Matthew Arnold's "Dover Beach." And it is this world, not another world out there beyond this one; this one, with all its pain, difficulty, evil, and misery, is "charged with the grandeur of God." If this is true, we must experience this real world, at least some times. Do we? That's the big question. Is it possible to believe in this real world? Or is Arnold right, that faith in such a world is no longer possible? For the remainder of this chapter, I want to speak to the question of our experience of the world.

What Is Our Experience of This World?

I believe in the real world described by Gerard Manley Hopkins and just outlined as the meaning of our faith in the resurrected Jesus of Nazareth. As a result, I have to believe that we can experience this real world. We do have experiences of this world as "charged with the grandeur of God." But we can easily pass them by as unimportant and miss their meaning. We need to be alert to experiences of the good news, ready to pay attention to them, to pay at least as much attention to these experiences as we do to bad news. It really is a question of paying attention to those experiences that reveal God's grandeur. It is the privilege and responsibility of pastoral ministers, especially spiritual directors, to help people to pay attention to such experiences.

Let me point to some such experiences that will, I hope, get you reflecting on your own experiences more positively. The first comes from a friend, Patrick Malone, SJ, who went to Haiti with a group delivering medicine to a health clinic. As the group was being driven to the clinic, they met a haggard woman asking for help. This incident reminded one of them, Marlene, of how awful she felt when she could not offer help or hope to a Haitian family on another trip. "One is so limited in the face of hardship and unfairness," she said, and continued, "The rural people here have a common saying in their language, Creole: *Bonjya konai*, "the good God knows." In a personal communication Pat Malone writes:

> When life is miserable, God knows, when one suffers, God knows. The whispered quote caused a slight movement of the other passengers' heads in Marlene's

direction. Without realizing the impact the phrase
had on them, Marlene had stirred something. . . .
Delivered in an inconsequential, matter-of-fact tone,
it had the same impact as the chimes used in Mass
when the priest raises the newly consecrated host.
Awaken. Do not speak; just stop whatever drifting
or self-absorption or pettiness is consuming you, so
you do not miss this symbol. Here, before your eyes,
you are invited to experience something that remains
both common and rare. Do not slumber past the significance. Do not dismiss it as ordinary, or easily
explainable.

That is a sign of hope in a very unlikely place indeed.

And I have found signs of hope in stories I've read. I
want to recount two such stories that lifted my spirits when
I read them. In his column in the *Boston Globe* on Tuesday,
March 4, 2003, Brian McGrory described a remarkable
instance of forgiveness. David, a young man on a motor-
cycle, was hit by a drunk driver and left a paraplegic who
needed around-the-clock care from his mother. The driver,
given the name Daniel in the article, had been arrested again
for drunk driving. David's brother went to the trial to see
that justice was done. Afterward he met Daniel and Daniel's
mother in the parking lot and stopped to tell them what
had happened to his brother since the accident. Daniel's

driving drunk again had been like a slap in the face to their family, he said, and then he suggested that Daniel come to visit his brother to see what he had done. Daniel and his mother decided to pay a visit. When Daniel saw his victim, he doubled over and began to sob uncontrollably. David's mother had wanted this moment for seven years, since the accident. But then, writes McGrory, "She couldn't help herself. She walked around the bed, walked up to the man who destroyed her son, and she hugged him." She said, "Daniel, it took a lot of guts to come here. It shows you have character. There's David. He has no future. But you do. You owe it to David and to your mother and to me and to yourself to fly right." Only God's grace could have produced such an act of forgiveness. The mother even begged McGrory not to use the young man's real name, believing that he could straighten out.

Matt Malone, SJ, no relative of Pat cited previously, wrote of a similar act of forgiveness in *America* on March 7, 2005. Matt's father, a firefighter, was awakened one night by an emergency call, a car wreck. The driver was OK, but the passenger was badly hurt, and Mr. Malone realized that it was his own son, Joseph, who died soon after. The driver was drunk. At the driver's trial Mr. Malone was asked to make a victim's statement just before sentencing. Usually such statements ask for the maximum sentence. Here is what Mr. Malone said:

My son Joseph was a bright, good-natured young man with enormous potential. The emotional impact of this event on my family has been devastating. Today the driver of the vehicle stands before you awaiting sentencing. He has admitted to his guilt. He was Joseph's friend and coworker; yet, through the thoughtlessness of his actions Joseph is dead. Kenny didn't approach that terrible night with the thought of harming anyone, least of all his friend, but the result is that one young man is dead, our family has suffered, and, not least of all, he himself has suffered. Kenny has to bear the knowledge of what he did for the rest of his life. That burden is far greater than any punishment this court could dispense. For this reason, I respectfully request that this court hear the appeal of the victim's parent and family and impose the minimum possible sentence. (19)

Matt Malone believes that his father was able to forgive Kenny because he was able, like Jesus, to see the human being in front of him. God's grace turned his heart to thoughts of forgiveness.

You will notice that these stories are not from pious sources. Of course, I could tell you stories of people for whom I act as a spiritual director, but then you might too easily write them off as something the elite experience. I wanted to use stories from ordinary life, because that's the point of this chapter; namely, God is found in surprising places and people. In fact, God can be found anywhere and at every moment. We need to pay attention to the good news, not just to the bad news that assaults us every evening on the nightly news and every day in our newspaper headlines. The world is charged with the grandeur of God. There is reason for hope in a dismal time, in fact at any time, because God has become one of us and shares our lives on this planet. God has a dream, a dream for this world of ours that is also God's own world.

And, remember, God is working to bring that dream about all the time. Reason for hope, indeed. And reason for us to do our best to get in tune with God's dream for our own happiness and for the good of our world.

9

Sage Advice for Times of Great Change

In *Stone Song: A Novel of the Life of Crazy Horse*, Win Blevins describes in poignant detail the terrible dilemma of the Lakota leader Crazy Horse as he and his people faced the end of their way of life with the coming of the white people. Until near the end of the novel Crazy Horse resists the forced restriction of his people to reservations. He and other Lakota see the coming of the white people as the end of an age—the age of the buffalo—and of their way of life as a nomadic people living off the buffalo. Just before his decision to enter the reservation for the sake of his people, he and another brave speak with his mentor, a seer named Horn Chips, who ruminates on how times change:

"Big changes come sometimes," he said. "Skan [spiritual vitality] circles, life circles. Not every seven generations, but seven times seven or a hundred times seven, changes come that are too great to foresee, far too great to understand." He looked at them somberly. "I believe this one of the teachings of the Inyan [Spirits]: When the old ways are dead," he said, "it means that a new way is upon us. We cannot discern it yet, but it is at hand. . . .

"I think we will not see the new way," Horn Chips said. "I think it will not become visible for seven generations. In that time the hoop of the people will seem to be broken, and the flowering tree will seem to be withered. But after seven generations some will see with the single eye that is the heart, and the new way will appear."

He looked directly at Crazy Horse. "The old way is beautiful. We turn backward to it and in taking leave we offer it our love. Then we turn forward and walk forth blindly, offering our love. Yes, blindly." (1995, 320–321)

Thus does Horn Chips counsel Crazy Horse to face the terrible changes before him and his people. I believe that he also gives good counsel to us—perhaps because the novel's author, besides having immersed himself in the Lakota culture, is immersed in our culture.

Our Time of Big Changes

We who have lived through any part of the twentieth century have experienced changes that go far beyond the ordinary. Horn Chips is correct. Sometimes changes come that are more far reaching and disorienting than ordinary. In such times, which can occasion severe anxiety, people cannot understand the changes or predict them. I believe that we are living in a time that is as revolutionary as any in history.

The twentieth century witnessed the upheaval of two world wars; the Holocaust (and similar horrors of attempted genocide); the cold war; the unbelievably rapid rise of technology; and the globalization of communications, the economy, and politics. Because of stupidity and scandals in high places, many have lost trust in our leaders as men and women of probity, integrity, and wisdom. Religious organizations have not been exempt from such mistrust. Those of us who are Catholics have seen our whole way of life change in the years since the Second Vatican Council. We have also experienced the scandal of the sexual abuse of minors by priests and religious and its attempted cover-up by bishops and religious superiors.

In addition, new philosophies have raised questions about the fundamentals of our knowledge and because of the mass media such questions have touched many educated men and women. How can we be sure that we know anything about our world? These events and trends have changed our world and our worldview in ways that were almost unimaginable a century ago.

I believe that the changes we have experienced in our lifetime have at least mildly traumatized most of us. We may not be fully aware of the trauma, but it is there. As we experience tensions and anxieties at the beginning of the new millennium, we need to have some sympathy for ourselves and others.

Guidelines for Coping with Big Changes

Let's see what Horn Chips' advice to Crazy Horse might say to us as we face these massive, unsettling changes. First, he notes that in such tumultuous times we cannot predict the way ahead: "changes come that are too great to foresee, far too great to understand." This is a hard saying. We feel that we, or at least those in charge, must be able to understand what is happening and know where we are going. Otherwise, we feel lost and disoriented. In addition, we want clarity about the future and some control over it.

In fact, however, no human being in history has clarity and control with regard to the future. The future, precisely as future, is unknowable. In all ages, not only in times of great change, men and women have had to walk forward into the future with hope and trust, not knowing precisely how things would turn out. This is all the more true in times such as those that confronted Crazy Horse and those that confront us. It might help to realize that Jesus of Nazareth himself had to go to his death on the cross in faith and hope and love, not knowing how, but trusting that his Father would bring light out of this darkness: "Father, into your hands I commend my spirit" (Luke 23:46).

Horn Chips says: "When the old ways are dead, it means that a new way is upon us. We cannot discern it yet, but it is at hand." This teaching of the Inyan (Spirits) is compatible with Judeo-Christian faith in a creator God whose Spirit acts in history. We are experiencing the demise of our social, cultural, and religious ways of life. The old ways are dead or dying. We must trust that our God continues to act to bring about the divine project.

In fact, we can take comfort in our Christian belief that, no matter what it looks like, God has done all that is needful for the salvation of the world in the life, death, and resurrection of Jesus of Nazareth. We are a people who believe that this world, because of its physical, biological, social, and spiritual ties with Jesus of Nazareth, is divinized, is inextricably united with the triune God. When cataclysmic changes occur in the world order, we must still believe that God's Spirit is with us, as Jesus promised: "When the Spirit of truth comes, he will guide you into all the truth (John 16:13). So when the old ways are dead, it means that a new way is upon us, even though we cannot discern it yet. This new way, however, will be consistent with what God has already accomplished through the life, death, and resurrection of Jesus and the sending of the Spirit.

"I think we will not see the new way," Horn Chips states. "I think it will not become visible for seven generations. In that time the hoop of the people will seem to be broken, and the flowering tree will seem to be withered." He is telling Crazy Horse that the new way will not be discernible in their lifetime—indeed, not for many lifetimes. Moreover it will seem that all is lost.

Faith Is Essential

In our day, many are tempted to despair. What have the life, death, and resurrection of Jesus actually accomplished as far as inaugurating the rule or kingship of God? The horrors that the twentieth and twenty-first centuries have spawned make it difficult to believe that God's Spirit is alive and active in our world. Indeed, it can seem as though God's plan has been thwarted, that God's kingdom has failed. "But," someone may argue, "God's rule is hidden and supernatural. It will only come about at the end of time in a cataclysmic judgment, in which the just shall be rewarded and the wicked punished."

This kind of otherworldly salvation, however, does not give much solace, nor does it do justice to the teaching and ministry of Jesus. He seems to have believed that the rule of God, which he inaugurated through his teaching and ministry, had something to do with the world as he knew it: "Go and tell John what you have seen and heard: the blind receive their sight, the lame walk, the lepers are cleansed, the deaf hear, the dead are raised, the poor have good news brought to them" (Luke 7:22). I do not believe that theories of another, supernatural realm, different from our own universe, fit with what Jesus preached and promised. In addition, such theories are not finally comforting or helpful; they will not assuage the anxieties that gnaw at the edges of our consciousness. The only way forward, I believe, is to allow these anxieties to rise into consciousness, to recognize that we are often near despair at the condition of our world and do wonder what God's coming to rule could possibly mean. It is at such times as this that our faith is tested. Do we believe in God, or do we not? Horn Chips' advice invites us to a similar kind of meditation as we made in the previous chapter.

When I entered the Society of Jesus in 1950, I almost did not need faith in God. The Roman Catholic Church and the Society of Jesus were thriving; seminaries and novitiates were packed; churches, schools, and retreat houses were being built and expanded at an unprecedented rate. We could believe in the success of the work of our hands without even being aware of it; we could believe in the church and, for Jesuits, in the Society of Jesus. But in the 1980s and 1990s, with the full realization of the impact of diminishment in the number of clergy and religious, we were faced with whether we really believed in God and in God's action in our world. I believe that we need to face the diminishment to know what faith in God really means. Just as Abraham had to believe that God would be faithful to his promises about Isaac even as he got ready to sacrifice him, just as Jesus had to believe that God would save Israel and the world through the shipwreck of his crucifixion, so too, we are called to believe that God's Spirit is still active in this world, in spite of appearances, and that God will reveal the new way to those who remain faithful.

"After seven generations," says Horn Chips, "some will see with the single eye that is the heart, and the new way will appear." This is our hope and our faith. We must believe that the new way to be a people who believe in the Resurrection in the changed circumstances of our age will be revealed to spiritually discerning men and women in time. Moreover, we must continually beg God to help us "see with the single eye that is the heart"—that is, to have discerning hearts, hearts that are disciplined enough to be able to discover the "rumor of angels" in these dark times. The new way may not be discerned in our time, but we must try to be alert for signs of its coming birth.

The Grace of Wisdom

"The old way is beautiful," observes Horn Chips. "We turn backward to it, and in taking leave we offer it our love." This is not easy advice to accept. To follow it is to accept that the old way is really dead or no longer works. When a way of life is threatened, we become anxious— sometimes very anxious. This way of life has given meaning to our lives, has sustained us through the ups and downs of life. It has also sustained our parents and grandparents and all those who have gone before us in our countries as well as in our churches and congregations. To admit that this way of life no longer works threatens our very selves and raises questions about the traditions handed down to us.

There are at least two tempting stances we can take toward such a threat. We can hold onto the old way for dear life, as though our very souls were at risk. For a long time Crazy Horse took this path. Or we can denigrate the old way, finding it benighted, naive, oppressive, or worse. Some of the Lakota leaders took this path.

The first stance, carried to excess, leads to nostalgia, an idealization of the past, and efforts to achieve its restoration. This traditionalist stance, which seems to have been taken by Archbishop Marcel-François Lefebvre and his followers, led to their estrangement from the Roman Catholic Church and his excommunication. It is a stance that many Christians who have not left their churches seem to have taken with some degree of belligerence. Before we write off people who adopt this stance, we might examine our own reactions to the great upheavals in our world and in our churches in the past thirty years. I, for one, can own up to experiencing at least occasional bouts of anxiety and doubt as I abandoned past practices of Roman Catholic piety—feelings prompted by the thought that I might be acting contrary to God's desire and design. That kind of anxiety and doubt can lead to adoption of the traditionalist stance.

The second stance, that of denigrating the old way, is no less a temptation and no less a way to deal with the anxieties brought on by the death of a way of life. Carried to excess, it leads to a wallowing in stories of the horrors of the past, to bitter resentment at what was done to "us" by those in charge, and to alienation from one's roots. Some former Catholics seem to be stuck in this stance. Again, before we write off people who take this stance, let's look into our hearts. I have to admit that I have found in myself tendencies toward this stance and have engaged in telling horror stories as though there had been nothing good in the old ways. Doesn't this stance underlie a kind of hidden delight at stories of scandal in the ranks of church leaders? It is not easy to follow Horn Chips' advice—that is, to recognize that the old way of life is indeed dead or dying, yet also to love it.

To move forward in faith, hope, and love, however, it is necessary to be able to follow that advice. I am reminded of Erik Erikson's final stage of development, which he characterizes as the crisis between despair and wisdom. Despair rises because we cannot accept the reality of who we are and have become. Wisdom means, as Erikson notes in *Childhood and Society*, "the acceptance of one's one and only life cycle as something that had to be and that, by necessity, permitted of no substitutions: it thus means a new, a different love of parents" (1963, 268).

It is important, I believe, to understand what Erikson is getting at. If, finally, I accept who I now am, warts and all, then I have accepted all that has happened to me and all that I have done in life, the good and the bad, because I am the product of everything that has happened to me and all that I have done. Moreover, I have also accepted my ancestry, all the saints and sinners who have contributed to who I am and to what I have become; I have accepted the ways of life that have influenced my ancestors and myself, with all their shortcomings and strong points.

The church came to such wisdom when it coined the phrase "O happy fault" to describe the sin of our first parents—a phrase sung during the Exultet of the Holy Saturday liturgy. I believe that this wisdom shines in the words of the resurrected Jesus to the two disciples on the road to Emmaus: "Was it not necessary that the Messiah should suffer these things and then enter into his glory?" (Luke 24:26). Jesus would not be the Messiah he now is if he had not suffered as he did. This does not mean that God decreed that the Messiah must suffer in this way; rather, it means that he would be a different Messiah if things had happened differently—if, for example, Israel had repented and believed the good news. To be who he now is, Jesus had to undergo the passion.

If we can attain or, rather, be given the grace of attaining such wisdom, then we can look back at our past way of life with love and take leave of it with love. If we are granted this grace, we will be freed from the debilitating resentment and anxiety that characterize us when we take either of the two stances described earlier.

10

We Had Hoped: Meditation in a Time of Crisis

I wrote this meditation for Easter 2004, at a time when the Roman Catholic Church in the United States was being buffeted by the sexual abuse crisis. It seems appropriate to include it in this series of meditations for use at any time when we are feeling down at the mouth. In addition it continues the reflection on the Emmaus story begun in the previous chapter.

The Catholic Church, which had stood so tall and proud after the Second World War and the election of the first Catholic as president, suffered some grievous blows in the years after 2002. There seemed no end to the tide of stories about the sexual abuse crisis. "When would the next bomb explode?" many of us asked, in our hearts, if not aloud. All of us felt the effects of this crisis. In addition, the effects of the precipitous drop in the number of diocesan seminarians and candidates for religious life, which began in the late 1960s, and the departure from the active priesthood and from religious congregations of thousands of members, which began at about the same time, were acutely felt, even in those areas of the country that had been rich in the number of both diocesan and religious priests and of religious sisters and brothers. Reeling from the sexual abuse stories, we now faced the prospect of closing parishes that had been the glory of the church in the past century. The most recent polls suggested that Protestants attend church weekly at a higher rate than Catholics. We had been brought low indeed from the glory days of the middle of the twentieth century.

How were we responding to these blows? Our reactions ran the gamut from sadness and depression to anger and resentment. I do not believe that one could characterize the mood of many meetings of Catholics, whether for Mass or for other events, as joyous and buoyant. There was heaviness in the atmosphere that betrayed sadness. In addition, many Catholics were angry. Clearly the most pained and angry were those who were abused and their families. But the sexual abuse crisis had probably angered us all, and the anger spread itself around at many targets. In addition, Catholics were polarized on many issues, and the positions seemed to be hardening as we tried to figure out what had happened to us as a people. Resentment was not far from the surface in many of us. How could this have happened to our church and to us? Resentment leads to the search for causes, for someone or something to blame. Vatican II? The sexual revolution? Permissiveness in seminaries and in society in general? Homosexual priests and bishops? Bishops who cared more for the reputation of the church than for the safety of children? The repression of emotions and feelings in the seminaries prior to Vatican II? Celibacy as a requirement for ordination? The failure to have women represented in the decision-making councils of the church? These reasons and many others had been adduced to explain what has happened to our church.

In this situation, with all these emotions acknowledged as present among us as a people, if not present in each one of us, I suggested a meditation on the Emmaus story in Luke 24:13–35. For the idea I am indebted to N. T. Wright, presently Anglican bishop of Durham, England, who offered such a meditation for the postmodern era in *The Challenge of Jesus: Rediscovering Who Jesus Was and Is*. Whenever we are buffeted by storms of doubt, anger, and resentment at the way the world or our circumstances are going we can make this meditation.

Luke 24:13–35

In Luke's Gospel we read a story of two disciples walking away from Jerusalem toward Emmaus on a Sunday morning. Some commentators believe they may have been a couple,

Cleopas and his wife. Jesus had been killed and buried on Friday. On Sunday morning they had heard that some women had found the tomb empty and had had a vision of angels saying that Jesus was alive. These two, however, had left Jerusalem for Emmaus without any hope. How could they have hope? They, like most of the people of Israel, believed that the Messiah would come to save God's people from their present status as an occupied and demeaned vassal of Rome and in the process begin the rule of God for the whole world. They and the other disciples had believed that Jesus was this Messiah. But then he had been cruelly and shamefully crucified and killed. There was no way that what had happened to Jesus could be put together with his being Messiah.

"We had hoped that he was the one to redeem Israel," they told the stranger they met on the road (Luke 24:21). Their hopes had been dashed on Friday. The Romans showed who had the power by killing Jesus in a degrading, humiliating way. God had done nothing to stop this naked display of power. So Jesus could not have been the Messiah. Despair took the place of hope in their hearts. The news about the empty tomb and the words of the angel did not break through the despair. "We had hoped, but there is no hope now."

As they walked the road to Emmaus, they must have been wondering what they would do now and may even have wondered whether the whole expectation of a Messiah was a pipe dream. Besides depression and sadness, could they have been filled with resentment as well, resentment that they had been taken in by Jesus, that their hopes had been so raised only to be dashed? Perhaps this explains why they had left Jerusalem and their other companions to return to Emmaus. They abandoned the community where they had been misled so badly, perhaps shaking the dust from their feet. Isn't that a normal human reaction to having one's hopes blown away? "I'm not going to get my hopes up again. You won't see me consorting with fools who believe in fairy tales."

Do you see yourselves in these two people? Can you empathize with them because you, too, had hoped? I suggest that we walk with them in imagination and allow our own feelings in this time of church crisis to surface. What are your feelings as you contemplate the situation of our church or any present troubling situation? Allow all the feelings to surface. They are your reality now, just as the feelings of the two disciples were their reality then.

A Retelling of the Story

After the disciples poured out their despair, their anger, their sadness, and their resentment to the stranger, he proceeded to tell them the story of Israel in such a way that the death of Jesus on the cross made sense—indeed, made the only possible sense of Israel's history. Luke does not give us the details of the stranger's discourse, but we can fill it in without too much difficulty.

Throughout Israel's history God had intervened to save the people when they were at their lowest ebb, brought to that point by their own sinful folly or that of their leaders. When they had no hope, God, once again, entered the picture and gave them hope.

Take one example from Israel's history. The prophet Ezekiel lived in the time of the Babylonian captivity when the Israelites had been carried off as slaves to Babylon and lived far from the Promised Land. The prophet is carried by the spirit to a valley filled with dead bones and is asked, "Mortal, can these bones live?" (Ezekiel 37:3). Of course, they cannot; they are dry and dead. But he is told to prophesy over the bones, "and they lived, and stood on their feet, a vast multitude." God then tells Ezekiel, "Mortal, these bones are the whole house of Israel. They say, 'Our bones are dried up, and our hope is lost; we are cut off completely.' Therefore, prophecy, and say to them, Thus says the Lord GOD: I am going to open your graves, and bring you up from your graves, O my people; and I will bring you back to the land of Israel" (Ezekiel 37:10–12). And bring them back God did.

Perhaps the stranger on the road to Emmaus retold such stories to these two disciples, reminding them that their faith is in God, and that God can bring the dead to life, can save the people even when all seems lost.

Burning Hearts

As the stranger told them the story, a story that included the death by crucifixion of Jesus, their hearts burned within them, but, apparently, they did not pay attention to this burning sensation until after Jesus broke bread with them at the end of their walk. Why were their hearts burning? I venture to say that the words of the stranger touched something deep within them. Let me explain.

They, like all of us, are created by God's desire, a desire that never fails, that is everlasting, that knows not death and can never be extinguished. That desire creates us, makes us who we are; indeed, it makes us desirable to God. And that desire lives deep inside us, drawing us to what God wants: namely, our friendship and union. That desire evokes hope in us, a hope that, no matter what happens, we are wanted by God and will live forever with God. The trauma of Jesus' cruel death had overwhelmed that hope for a while, but the words of the stranger on the road stoked the fire of that hope again. When they reached Emmaus, they did not want to let the stranger go and prevailed on him to have dinner with them.

In the breaking of the bread they recognized who the stranger was and then realized that their hearts had been burning as he told them the story. Death had not triumphed; it had no sting. The Crucifixion was, indeed, the paradoxical victory of God. They hurried back to the community in Jerusalem, where they found that their companions also had good news to match theirs; they, too, who had hoped now radiated hope and joy.

In any time of trial and the crash of hope this story can be good news for us too. But we need to let it touch us where we are, in our sadness, our anger, our resentment. Let's invite the stranger, who is no stranger, to tell us the story that will set our hearts burning again.

PART IV

On God and God's Desire

✧

When we engage in a relationship with God, we learn something about ourselves. We learn that we have fallen short of God's dreams for us and our world. But we also learn that God's love for us and desire for our good does not change with our failures. God still pursues us. As we reflect on our relationship with God, therefore, we learn something about God. In the following chapters I offer you some meditations on what we might learn about God from engaging in the relationship of friendship God wants.

✧

11

God as Dance

This meditation seems to fit well after the section on discernment and as we begin some meditations on God, even though I begin it with the realization that many people have problems with the pronouns and personal names we use to refer to God. See how it strikes you.

The feminist movement has made many of us conscious of the almost exclusively male language used with regard to God. In fact, of course, God is neither male nor female; God is Mystery, the Nameless One. Thomas Aquinas asserts that we must deny, almost in the same breath, every positive statement we make about God. Whether with tongue in cheek or not, the novelist Graham Greene, in a letter to the editor of *The Tablet* some years ago, suggested using the neuter to refer to God, a suggestion that has not met with overwhelming favor. I believe that the problem is rooted precisely in the experience of the Mystery we call God. When we encounter God we have no problem at all addressing God in the second person, as *you*, but no third-person pronoun for the God addressed is adequate to the experience.

God Is Personal

Two sessions of spiritual direction gave me some insight that may prove helpful to others. One man said that his experience of God was not personal. Yet when he spoke about his times of prayer, I noted that he acted in a personal way toward God. He let God know of his concerns and interests and felt God's presence. In other words, he acted like a person in the presence of another person. What he meant, we concluded, was that God was not a person in the same sense as his own father or a friend.

The other person said that God seemed like a dance. Yet she also acted personally toward this "dance." She felt that God loved her and had freed her from self-destruction. She was grateful to God and felt warmth toward God. Once a book reviewer mentioned a remark by the German philosopher Oswald Spengler that music is the only art that can convey the idea of God. Let us reflect together on how we experience the Mystery we call God.

In Tune with God or Out of Tune

Often I have described experiences of great well-being accompanied by a strong desire for "I know not what" and indicated that people who have such experiences may be experiencing their own creation as the apple of God's eye. When we have such an experience, we spontaneously feel gratitude and praise. The response is personal, although we do not experience God precisely as a person like any other we know. One desires "I know not what," the all. Yet almost without thought we respond to a "you." For example, we want to say "Thank you." Can you recall such experiences?

Sometimes we experience ourselves on top of our game, as it were. A number of years ago, for a period of about two weeks, I had such an experience. I felt in the flow, lived in the present without much concern for the past or the future. I was very present to people I met, uncannily aware of how they were feeling. I was not worried about whether I was in the right place or had done the right things. I experienced the mystery of things and people. People remarked that they sensed something larger than ordinary life when with me. I recall being on an airplane and hearing a baby crying; I knew that the baby's ears were pained by the pressure of the cabin, and I felt God's presence as a soothing presence for the child. I felt grateful during this time, felt in tune with God. But God was not a person I could imagine. Yet I addressed God as "You."

Sometimes we experience ourselves as out of sorts, not right with the world, the opposite of in the flow. We may attribute the feelings to an upset stomach, to the weather, to poor sleep. But often enough when I have reflected on such experiences in myself, I have discovered that I do not feel in tune with my best self, my ideals, my hopes; there is something gnawing at my conscience, or I am avoiding an honest look at a particular situation in my life. For example, at some level I may know that there is something wrong in the way I am relating to my best friend, but I am afraid to look honestly at the relationship. In such circumstances, I believe, I experience God too. My spontaneous response, once I let myself become aware of the malaise, is to ask for help to face what is wrong, again addressing the Mystery as "You."

As I mentioned earlier, John Macmurray has developed the notion of the creation of the universe as the one action of God. God is creating a universe, and God's intention for this one action, it seems from revelation, is that it be an environment where all human beings can live in community with God and thus as brothers and sisters of one another in harmony with the whole of creation. Our actions can be in tune or out of tune with God's one action. If they are in tune, we will know it by the sense of satisfaction and inner and outer harmony we experience. Ignatius of Loyola would call such an experience "consolation." If our actions are not in tune, then we will experience ourselves as frustrated and unhappy. Ignatius would call such an experience "desolation."

Could it not be that when we experience the sense of well-being and the strong desire for "I know not what," we are experiencing the creative action of God? Could it not be that when we are in tune with God's one action we are experiencing what I described as being in the flow? In *Gift from the Sea* Anne Morrow Lindbergh likens a good relationship to a dance. It is, she says,

> built on some of the same rules. The partners do not need to hold on tightly, because . . . they know they are moving to the same rhythm, creating a pattern together, and being invisibly nourished by it. The joy of such a pattern is not only the joy of creation or the joy of participation, it is also the joy of living in the moment. (1955, 104)

This description of a good relationship seems to fit our experience of God when we are in tune with God's one intention, living as much as possible as brothers and sisters of Jesus. And the description of being a clumsy dancer seems to fit our experience when we are out of tune with God's one intention. Moreover, these descriptions strike me as coinciding remarkably well with what Ignatius describes as consolation and desolation.

The Triune God

Christians believe that God is triune, that there are three "persons" in God. What theologians say of the three Persons is that the only quality that distinguishes them from one another is their mutual relationships. Perhaps to describe this mutuality of relationships the best metaphor is the dance. Quite apart from creation, in other words, the one God is dance: Father, Son, and Holy Spirit so perfectly related that nothing separates them except their relations. It may even be that the pain we experience when we love someone deeply, yet cannot be perfectly one with him or her, is another indication that we are made in the image and likeness of God where such union is the reality.

To say that God is experienced as the music to which we dance, indeed, as dance itself, may sound impersonal. But the music, the dance, we address as "You." The Mystery, the Nameless One, is You to my I. Indeed, Jesus named the Mystery *Abba*, "dear Father." The experience of God that we have cannot be fully captured by imaginative language such as *Father, Mother, Lover, Friend*. Yet we address the Mystery as "You," and we feel toward this You as we feel toward the best father, mother, lover, we could ever imagine. Indeed, because interpersonal relationships are what make us human and people at all, we must use such metaphorical language taken from our highest development to speak of the encounter with God. What is most amazing about human life in this mysterious cosmos, we find through experience, is that it is homelike, familial, that there is an interpersonal quality about it that gives us security in spite of the vast spaces and seeming voids we inhabit; spontaneously we speak in personal terms to the Mystery that surrounds us.

Care with Our God Language

There is no help for the problem of how to refer to God when describing our experience of God to others or when doing theology or catechesis. No predicates or third-person pronouns can adequately capture the Mystery we have encountered. But we can be careful and considerate of one another's sensibilities. The feminist movement has done us all a service by bringing to our attention what it means to women always to hear God referred to as a male. While we will always have difficulties with the third person in referring to God, most believers have no difficulty at all acting personally toward God and using the second person when they encounter the divine Mystery. Saying "you" seems the only appropriate language.

12

Who God Is and How God Wants Us to Develop

In the previous chapters we have reflected on some of the effects of engaging in a relationship of friendship with God. In this chapter I want to present some thoughts on the kind of human development God wants. What does God desire for us as we develop as human beings?

In *The Joy of Being Wrong*, an original and dense theological work on, of all things, original sin, James Alison uses the anthropology of René Girard to develop his theology of original sin. Alison takes the stance that we cannot understand the doctrine of original sin or, for that matter, any Christian doctrine, unless we, like the first disciples, begin with the experience of the resurrected Jesus. The New Testament's first concern, he maintains, is "an announcement about God."

"The resurrection of Jesus was not a miraculous event within a preexisting framework of understanding of God, but the event by which God recast the possibility of human understanding of God" (1998, 115). In other words, we learn who God is through the death and resurrection of Jesus.

N. T. Wright, presently Anglican bishop of Durham, England, makes a similar point in an article in *Bible Review*, where he argues that much of theology had started with an oppressive notion of God into which it tried to fit Jesus, thus producing

> a Jesus who only seems to be truly human, but in fact is not. My proposal is not that we know what the word "God" means, and manage somehow to fit Jesus into that. Instead, I suggest that we think historically about a young Jew, possessed of a desperately risky, indeed apparently crazy, vocation, riding into Jerusalem, denouncing the Temple, dining once more with his friends, and dying on a Roman cross— and that we somehow allow our meaning of the word "God" to be re-centered on that point.

Wright would agree with Alison that we need to include the experience of the Resurrection to know what the word *God* means. Both authors state emphatically that we can only understand God, insofar as we can understand God at all, from the vantage point of the historical human being, Jesus of Nazareth, and specifically of his death by crucifixion and his resurrection. From this same vantage point, I believe, we can understand the kind of human development God wants.

The Easter Experience

What did the first disciples experience with Easter? In chapter 10 we contemplated the story of the two disciples on the road to Emmaus (Luke 24:13–35). They had hoped that Jesus was the Messiah who would lead Israel out of bondage to Gentile rulers. More than that, their hope for the Messiah, like the hope of Israel as a people, was not just hope for Israel alone, but for the whole world. With the coming of the Messiah Israel's vocation to be the light to the Gentiles would be fulfilled, and all peoples would stream to worship the one true God, the God who had chosen Israel for this very vocation. For the disciples these hopes had been dashed when Jesus died the humiliating, demeaning death of a criminal on a Roman cross.

It is important for our understanding of their despair to realize that there had been Jews who considered themselves the Messiah (and who were considered by influential religious leaders to be the Messiah) during the century before and the one after the time of Jesus. Their deaths, most by crucifixion, were proof that each was not the Messiah. The disciples had no category of "crucified Messiah"; these two words could not coexist. In addition, Jesus died as a despised, degraded victim. With this kind of cruel judicial murder Rome showed its vassals who was boss, in effect saying, "You are of no account to us. We have the power; you are nothing." Such a degrading death could not have been the victory of God that the Messiah was supposed to inaugurate. No wonder that these disciples could say to the stranger they met on the road, "We had hoped." Their hopes were now as dead as was Jesus himself.

This stranger, however, proceeded to tell them the story of Israel in a way that made sense of this seeming debacle. It was a revolutionary telling of the story, but one that had been hinted at by the prophets, especially in the songs of the Suffering Servant of the prophet Isaiah. It took some time for the full impact of his retelling of the story to sink in, leading to the development of Christian theology. Each generation of Christians, indeed each Christian, needs to assimilate the story, and its full impact and meaning are never exhausted. The implications of the experience, in faith, of the resurrection of Jesus have relevance to our understanding of human development, a relevance that goes hand in hand with a deeper understanding of who God is.

Meaning for Human Development: Death Has No Sting

The disciples experienced something extraordinary. In *history*, a human being who had been cruelly put to death was raised from death to live forever. Death no longer had dominion over him, and according to him, over anyone who believed in him. "Very truly, I tell you, whoever believes has eternal life" (John 6:47). Prior to the death and resurrection of Jesus there were intimations that the dead lived on, but there was no experience that could be pointed to as grounds for this belief. Moreover, those Jews who believed in the resurrection of the dead believed that it would come only with the new age brought in by God's Messiah when all the dead would rise together. Now the disciples experienced the same man, who had lived with them and who had died on the cross, as alive and acting in history.

Moreover, Jesus' continued existence as a human being was different from the continued existence of Lazarus or the daughter of Jairus, whom Jesus had raised from the dead, both of whom, we presume, lived ordinary lives until their second death. Jesus appeared and disappeared at will, for one thing, and seemed to move through space and time in unusual ways. He was not immediately recognized until he made some familiar gesture or called a name. Finally, he did not die again but disappeared from their sight, promising the gift of the Spirit who would make his presence available to people until the end of time, a promise fulfilled at Pentecost.

As the disciples took in these extraordinary experiences and reflected on them, they became less and less afraid of persecution and of death. For example, in Acts we read that Peter and the apostles, after they had been flogged, "rejoiced that they were considered worthy to suffer dishonour for the sake of the name" (Acts 5:41). These were the same apostles who had cowered behind closed doors after the crucifixion of Jesus. And of Stephen, as he was being stoned to death, we read, "He prayed, 'Lord Jesus, receive my spirit'" and then "Lord, do not hold this sin against them" (Acts 7:59–60). Faith in Jesus mitigates or removes, it seems, debilitating fear of pain and even of death. This kind of faith led Paul to cry out:

> When this perishable body puts on imperishability, and this mortal body puts on immortality, then the saying that is written will be fulfilled: "Death has been swallowed up in victory." "Where, O death, is your victory? Where, O death, is your sting?" The sting of death is sin, and the power of sin is the law. But thanks be to God, who gives us the victory through our Lord Jesus Christ. (1 Corinthians 15:54–57)

As a result of the experience of Jesus' resurrection, the disciples came to a deeper understanding of God the Creator. God creates us to live forever, and somehow bodily. Faith, of course, is required, but it is a faith grounded in the experience of the first disciples who saw and believed. Jesus lives as a human being beyond death and tells us that such living is ours as well as his. Human development means a growth in trust of God's gift of life as eternal leading to a mitigation of the fear of death.

God Is Forgiving Love

The disciples also discovered that Jesus, who had, on the cross, forgiven his torturers, now demonstrated his forgiveness and continuing love and friendship for his friends who had abandoned and denied him. Moreover, he gave them the power to forgive other's sins in his name. God was not only gratuitous love but also forgiving love. God even forgives those who abandoned, denied, or killed the beloved Son. If God could forgive such sins, then nothing could separate human beings from God's love except the absolute refusal of that love. And even then God's love would not change.

No one who experienced such forgiveness in Jesus could any longer define God as one who condemns those who do not toe the line, do not follow the commandments exactly. Human beings are not put into this world to fulfill

God's willful commands. Whatever the tree of the knowledge of good and evil of Eden meant, it did not mean an arbitrary demand from a God who could not countenance rivals as the serpent insinuated: "You will not die; for God knows that when you eat of it your eyes will be opened, and you will be like God, knowing good and evil" (Genesis 3:4–5). God cannot be defined in any way as a rival of human beings or concerned about such rivalry. God is gratuitous and forgiving love. The human development God wants is growth in the acceptance of God's desire to forgive us, no matter what we have done, and growth in the trust that God is not a demanding tyrant.

God Wants Us to Love One Another and Makes It Possible

These early disciples, who had during Jesus' life, and perhaps immediately after his death, been caught in relationships of mistrust and rivalry toward one another (see Mark 9:33–37; 10:35–45), found in themselves a love for one another that must have mystified them at first.

Now, after the descent of the Spirit, these same disciples and their new converts are depicted in this way:

> Now the whole group of those who believed were
> of one heart and soul, and no one claimed private

ownership of any possessions, but everything they
owned was held in common. With great power the
apostles gave their testimony to the resurrection of
the Lord Jesus, and great grace was upon them all.
There was not a needy person among them, for as
many as owned lands or houses sold them and brought
the proceeds of what was sold. They laid it at the
apostles' feet, and it was distributed to each as any had
need. There was a Levite, a native of Cyprus, Joseph,
to whom the apostles gave the name Barnabas (which
means "son of encouragement"). He sold a field that
belonged to him, then brought the money, and laid it
at the apostles' feet. (Acts 4:32–37)

Admittedly this depiction may be idealized, but it does point
to some reality in the early Christian community that was
very different from what had gone on before. These early
Christians found themselves not only not engaged in rivalry
with one another but also not acquisitive and hoarding,
indeed, spontaneously generous in giving and receiving.

Moreover, the early Christians were distinguished by
their love for one another, so much so that this love became
a witness to the truth of their beliefs as Tertullian (circa A.D.
200) claimed: "It is our care of the helpless, our practice of
loving kindness that brands us in the eyes of many of our
opponents. 'Only look,' they say, 'look how they love one

another!'" In his sociological study *The Rise of Christianity*, Rodney Stark (who cites Tertullian's statement, p. 87) maintains that one of the causes of the spectacular rise of Christianity in a few short centuries was this love for one another. The linking of love of God with love of neighbor in Judeo-Christian thought and action was revolutionary, he says. These assertions underline the supposition of this chapter; namely, that a new or at least deepened understanding of God and of human beings came into the world with the life, death, and resurrection of Jesus. Even more, what came into the world was the communal belief that it was possible to live the way of Jesus and the communal practice of that way. The human development God wants is growth in the ability to love one another.

The Trinity and Human Relationships

In the light of the Resurrection the early Christians came to realize that God is intrinsically relational, and that, because of who God is, we, too, are intrinsically relational. The doctrine of the Trinity was only gradually elaborated, but very early Christians recognized that the One whom Jesus called Father, Jesus himself, and the Spirit who enlivened Christians are one God, yet distinct from and in relation to one another. The three are so united in their mutual relationships that these relationships are the One Mystery we call God. There is no rivalry among them; they love one another absolutely.

Human beings are made in the image and likeness of the triune God. With the faith-inspired experience of the life, death, and resurrection of Jesus, Christians came to understand that human beings were intrinsically relational and called, from the beginning, to be like God in their relationships. This is the kind of human development God wants.

What We Are Saved From

Now we turn to the realization of the early Christians that they had been saved from something that contaminated their lives and the lives of everyone else in the world, namely from what Paul, in Romans 5, calls the effects of the sin of Adam. Earlier Paul had written that "all have sinned and fall short of the glory of God; they are now justified by his grace as a gift, through the redemption that is in Christ Jesus" (Romans 3:23–24). Because of the salvation they had received and were experiencing in faith the early Christians realized that they and all human beings had been in a sinful state. As Alison remarks, "the content of original sin is known only in the process of its forgiveness" (*Faith Beyond Resentment*, 1998, 140). From what are we being saved? If we can only know its content as we are forgiven it, then we see the contours of original sin as we allow ourselves to be embraced by the saving grace of Jesus Christ. The experience, in faith, of his life, death, and resurrection saves us from a crippling and ultimately sinful relationship with God, with one another, and with the universe.

From Rivalry with God

We human beings want to be like God, to be deathless, but we want it not as the gift that it is, but as something that we grasp and control. The serpent's words to Eve tempt her to try to do this. Notice that our grasping for likeness to God is based on the fear that we cannot have it unless we grasp it. We act as though we were in a rivalrous relationship with God. But the experience of salvation reveals to us that what we are grasping at has been freely given because God is gratuitous love. God desires us into being precisely so that we can be like God, so that we can be friends of God, so that we can live forever. Insofar as we believe in the God revealed by Jesus, we are freed of fear and can accept being and life and everything else as the gratuitous gifts they are. "There is no fear in love, but perfect love casts out fear; for fear has to do with punishment, and whoever fears has not reached perfection in love. We love because he first loved us" (1 John 4:18–19).

From Rivalry with One Another

In addition, our experience of the salvation wrought by Jesus frees us to love one another and reveals that the boundaries of such love cannot be set anywhere short of the whole human race. We recognize, as we are being saved, that we are no different from others, that we all fall short of what God hopes for us in our relationships with God, with one another, and with the universe. When, for example, I look into the eyes of Jesus on the cross and hear him say, "Father, forgive them; for they do not know what they are doing," I know that he means me, too, not just those who are actually crucifying him (Luke 23:24). I, too, have sinned and fallen short; I have been craven and cowardly and fearful enough so that I might well have been one of his crucifiers or his betrayer had I been there. I am just as much in need of his forgiveness as is any other human being, and if I have been kept from the worst that our kind can do, it is only by the grace of God. My brothers and sisters in complicity are everywhere, and all of us are equally offered the forgiving love of God, are God's beloved sons and daughters who have gone astray. I cannot exclude anyone from that circle because God does not exclude anyone from it. The only way someone can get out of that circle is by self-exclusion, by refusing the love and forgiveness offered and doing it definitively and forever, an awful risk that God takes in creating us in God's own image.

From the Need of Scapegoats

From this point of view we are also freed from the search for someone else to blame for our plight. From the story of the first man and woman in Genesis on, we humans have been trying to foist the blame for what has gone wrong on others. Adam blames Eve; Eve blames the serpent. We all want to shirk our own complicity in the sinful state of our world. In doing so we often look for scapegoats and make them bear our guilt, as the Israelites did with a real goat in the desert. This search for someone else to blame leads to bigotry, to stigmatization, and, taken to its full extent, to such horrors as the "final solution" of the Holocaust, the killing fields of Cambodia, and the appalling genocide in Rwanda, all of which we witnessed in the past century alone. Jesus died because of this search for a scapegoat, among other reasons. Caiaphas, the high priest, cried out to those who were trying to protect Jesus, "You know nothing at all! You do not understand that it is better for you to have one man die for the people than to have the whole nation destroyed" (John 11:49–50). Jesus, God's own Son, was the ultimate scapegoat. The search for scapegoats is part of the sinful state from which we have been saved.

From Individualism

What we realize as we are freed to love our fellow human beings is that we have been living out of tune with the creative desire of God that brings us into being to live in love with one another. We realize that our relationships are problematic because they are based not on love for others but on fear for ourselves. Fear for oneself leads ultimately to an individualism contrary to God's triune being in whose image we are created.

A Note on Concupiscence

The effects of the sin of Adam still reside in us in a tendency to revert to those ways of understanding life and of living it that are out of tune with God's nature and with God's dream in creating us. Theologians have called this effect of original sin "concupiscence," a tendency to fall short of the glory of God. But we have the possibility of continual conversion from this effect because the Holy Spirit has been given to us. We can, by the grace of the Spirit, develop into the kind of human beings God desires. We are called to develop into "friends of God and prophets" (Wisdom 7:27) in the image of Jesus, and we are given the grace to do so.

Conclusion

Two final comments are in order. First, we become friends of anyone only by entering into a trusting, transparent relationship with that person. In the course of growing in friendship, friends develop shared values, dreams, and hopes. They become like one another, in other words. To develop into friends of God in the image of Jesus we need to engage in such a relationship of trust and transparency with Jesus and with his Father. Such an engagement is called prayer. As we get to know and love Jesus more, we grow in likeness to him and thus in likeness to God.

The second comment has to do with the reach of this notion of human development. What we Christians believe is not some arcane doctrine that has relevance only to us. No, our God is the one true God, and Jesus of Nazareth, a historical person, is the Son of God raised bodily from the dead. In other words, we believe that in Jesus God is present to, incarnated in, humanity eternally. What Gerard Manley Hopkins wrote is literally true: "The world *is* charged with the grandeur of God" (italics mine). God creates our world to call all human beings to the kind of human development modeled for us by Jesus. This kind of human development is hope for the whole world. We are called to be friends of God, and prophets to our world of this hope. But it would be foreign to the way of Jesus to try to force our beliefs on others. We must do what the early Christians did, witness to the truth about this real world with our words, but especially with our lives.

13

How God Reacts to Us

At the end of Brian Moore's novel *Black Robe*, the Jesuit priest Père Laforgue is baptizing Hurons in French Canada knowing that their baptism will mean the end of their civilization. He has witnessed the tragic clash of alien cultures in colonial French Canada; has himself been tortured by Native Americans; and has, at times, wondered about the existence of God. The novel ends with these words: "And a prayer came to him, a true prayer at last. 'Spare them. Spare them, O Lord. Do you love us?' 'Yes.'" (1997, 256). With these few words the novelist captures one of the deepest desires of the human heart, to know in our bones that God loves us, singly and as a whole. We want to know that God reacts favorably to us even though we feel as profoundly broken or sinful as Père Laforgue. But how do we know that the voice Laforgue hears, or the voice we hear, is actually the voice of God? Reflection on some experiences helps me realize how we discern the reactions of God in our ordinary experience. I hope that they will help you.

On the morning of November 16, 1989, I received a telephone call telling me of the brutal murder of six Jesuit priests, their cook, and her daughter in El Salvador. Every time that I let the images of those murdered men and women touch me, I felt a sense of horror and revulsion, an involuntary turn of my head as if to ward off the sight. My blood began to boil and an almost-murderous rage rose in me as I imagined the killers. Even now as I write these lines, I experience some of the same wave of feelings and emotions. At a memorial Mass for them I wept openly a few times, and at the end of the Mass I could hardly speak my thanks to all who participated because I became so choked up with a mixture of emotions.

That same day I took four students from Boston College on an overnight retreat. We were going to spend time in private prayer to ask God to help us experience our own and the world's creation and God's dream for us. Over the course of the afternoon, evening, and next morning we spent three hours in private prayer, and after each prayer session we got together to talk about what happened during our time of prayer. Just before one of the prayer sessions I found out that my niece had given birth to her first child,

Cara Anne. With Psalm 139 as a background I began to pray. I imagined my niece and her husband holding their daughter in their arms, just marveling at the wonder of her. Suddenly I thought that this image is only a pale image of God's delight in Cara Anne and every baby born into this world. I was close to tears as I felt the welling up of a love and desire that seemed immeasurably more than my heart could hold. God's desire brings Cara Anne and every other human being into existence. How breathtakingly precious each of us is to God! I could not doubt that I was experiencing something of God's reaction to each precious life on this planet.

My thoughts turned to the horrors in El Salvador that very day. Eight of God's precious children had had their lives brutally snuffed out and their bodies desecrated. How does God react to such horror? I felt again some of the same emotions I described earlier. After the centuries of human cruelty God has witnessed, I wonder whether my shock reflects God's reaction; perhaps God still frowns in incomprehension (figuratively) at human inhumanity.

But what about my murderous rage at the killers, my desire for vengeance? Are these emotions a reflection of God's reaction? Does God want vengeance? For some reason these emotions did not last long. I wanted the cycle of revenge and murder to stop; I did not want to have any part in continuing it. I was almost overcome again by an immense sorrow and pain and felt welling up in me a cry of anguish, as though God were saying: "This is not what I intend. I want all those whom I desire into life to live as brothers and sisters, and look what they do to one another." My rage and desire for revenge faded into the background. The killers, for their own salvation, will have to acknowledge what they have done and live with their guilt, but, I believe, God does not want vengeance. "An eye for an eye" is not God's value. I believe that I experienced something of God's reaction to the brutality and inhumanity of human beings who, in spite of all that, are still precious in God's eyes.

The students also had their experiences of God and shared them in the group. One young woman said that a feeling of great peace washed over her as she read the first lines of Psalm 139: "O Lord, you have searched me and known me. / You know when I sit down and when I rise up; / you discern my thoughts from far away. / You search out my path and my lying down, / and are acquainted with all my ways." She felt safe, no longer anxious and self-concerned. Other students also felt buoyed up by and elated at the notion that God had great dreams for each of them, wanted the best for them. They also felt some fear of what God might desire for them, fear of the unknown and of the challenge. As they talked, they had no doubt that they had experienced God's reactions to them. Nor did I doubt it.

In fact, after the third prayer session one of the students voiced her discomfort, and even irritation, that God seemed so willing to forgive and take her and all of us back into good terms without exacting a price. I took this reaction as another indication that she was encountering God and not her own projections. We are brought up on conditional love and do not know how to deal with God's unconditional love. We expect to have to earn love and forgiveness, not to receive them as gratuitous gifts. Jesus describes God's reaction in the parable of the prodigal son, which is really the story of the prodigal father (Luke 15:11–32). Often enough our reaction is that of the elder son in that same parable, the expectation that our relationship with God is on a quid pro quo basis.

As we talked about our experiences in prayer, I felt deeply happy and in admiration of the goodness of these young men and women who so easily shared with one another their experiences of God. As I reflected on my reactions, I again came to the conclusion that God was revealing delight in these conversations and in us who took our relationship with God so seriously.

The outpouring of sympathy and compassion for the martyrs in El Salvador and for the poor people of that ravaged country struck me as another indication of God's reactions to us. People were experiencing the gift of God's Holy

Spirit drawing us to compassion and solidarity with all those who suffer. We Jesuits were surprised at how many people of all walks of life took the time to write or speak a word of sympathy and solidarity with us. One of the most touching letters was addressed to the Jesuit community by four students at Boston College. In part they said: "Through our interaction with the Jesuit community at Boston College we have come to feel a part of the Jesuit family. These priests, like the Jesuits at Boston College, exemplified their ideal of service to others through their commitment to education for faith, peace, and justice. Their death has left us with an ever stronger sense of their mission which we wish to follow. We have come to feel a part of the Jesuit Society and so we stand in solidarity with you in this time of pain."

Here, too, I sense in their words an echo of God's reaction to this appalling situation, God drawing us together into one family.

Finally, a few days later, someone who was deeply moved by the assassinations told me that she had had an experience of overpowering love for the people of El Salvador. Images of various faces passed before her inner eye, and she was filled with love and compassion for them and for all humankind. It was almost more than her heart could bear. She was convinced that she had experienced in some pale way God's own reactions to the sufferings of human beings.

I believe that we can come to know through experience, and not just through theological reflection, God's reactions to us. The experiences I have reflected on in this essay are not foreign to any of us. We only need to pay attention to our reactions to life around us, and we will come to discern in our experience God's own reactions to that life and to us. "Do you love us?" "Yes."

PART V

On the Impact on Us of Friendship with God

✧

When we relate in friendship with God, we learn something not only about God but also about ourselves. In this final section I have collected some meditations on what we learn about ourselves. I hope that they help you in your friendship with God. Perhaps they will also spark insights of your own that come from your engagement with God.

✧

14

Changing Our Image of God

The words "God loves us" roll rather easily off the tongue but do not seem to lead, for most of us, to instinctive reactions of joy and excitement when we think of God. Yet these are our instinctive reactions in the presence of someone who, we are sure, loves us. I once saw a picture of young children taken just after someone had said, "Let us pray." Their faces and bodies were contorted, their hands folded tightly. Some looked down, and some up in the air. The picture was shown to evoke a smile, and it did. But it also pained me when I reflected on it. These children did not look as though they had just heard a call to meet someone who loved them very much. What would be the result in later life?

I find that in my unguarded moments I have a default image of God. I take the idea of a default from computer usage, in which the default setting is the one that automatically comes up unless one specifies something else. For instance, on my word processor the default font is Times New Roman and the default type size is twelve points. The word processor automatically uses these defaults unless I specify otherwise. When I speak of a default image of God, I refer to the self-God image that colors my spontaneous reactions to the mention of God.

Almost without thinking, I tend to beg for forgiveness for my past sins or to ask for favors, and I cringe interiorly when I imagine God knowing everything about me. So my spontaneous image of God does not feature what I have often seen in loving parents, namely, sheer delight in their children, and, at least when they are adults, enjoyment of their company. I do not, it seems, transfer that image to God, at least as a default position. My default seems more like God wagging a finger of blame at me, or at least looking at me with some unhappiness.

Many people have a similar default image of God, perhaps the result of the same kind of teaching that led the children in the picture to go into contortions of face and body when they heard the words, "Let us pray." So while the words "God loves us" may slide easily off the tongue, they don't seem to have much of an impact on how we spontaneously relate to God. What are the reasons for this default and its persistence, and how can we change it?

The Default Self-God Image

Growing up all of us develop ways of making sense of our world. These ways are structures or patterns that reduce anxiety and enable us to function in a very complex world. Among these psychological structures are patterns that help us to deal with interpersonal relations. Our initial reactions to new people we meet are partly conditioned by such patterns that we have learned since childhood. These patterns of self in relation to others could be called our defaults for making sense of ourselves in relation to others. These default patterns work, for the most part, without our awareness.

We also develop such a default pattern of self in relation with God, a pattern that derives from and, as a result, is colored by the self-other patterns we have developed over the course of our lives in dealing with significant other people. Thus, our relations with our parents and other significant authority figures of childhood affect our way of relating to God.

In addition, we began developing this self-God pattern when we were first introduced to the idea of God, and thus it is colored by the images of God taught to us in childhood and by how we, as children, internalized these notions and images. Our default pattern of self in relation with God has, therefore, like all our patterns for self-other relationships, some rather primitive features. Moreover, many of us have not allowed the self-God pattern much room for development in our later lives. Hence, many of us walk around with a default that is still rather undeveloped. This default can be idolatrous because it is so far from the reality of who God is and wants to be for us.

Because it developed when we were very young, it may be very difficult to change. The self-God pattern we develop is a way to make sense of the great mysteries of life on this earth, especially the mysteries of accident, pain, loss, and death. Why we exist at all is one of the fundamental questions that confront anyone who becomes aware of the fragility of life on this planet. Children become aware of this fragility through the death of pets, of siblings, of grandparents, of friends. God is often invoked as the one who causes these deaths. Children can internalize some terrible images of God as a result. Often, too, adults try to soften the blow to children by such statements as, "God took Nana because he loves her." The child is left to wonder who will be the next person God will take from him or her because of this love. But more fundamentally, God is invoked to make sense of these terrible events and to soothe the anxiety connected with them. Patterns developed to deal with strong anxiety tend to be relatively rigid and hard to change.

Because the self-God pattern of relationship is reinforced, often enough, by authoritative church teaching, it may be even harder to change. To change an image of God learned in childhood can seem dangerous to our faith in God. In addition, many of us, even those who go on to higher education, may not have had our image of God challenged much at all because we have not engaged in any theological or religious learning since childhood. The analogy with a default on a computer limps in this instance because the default image of God cannot be changed by pressing a button or just by desiring it.

Changing the Default

So the question arises, "How can we change the default?" We need to begin with one clear fact; namely, that our God image will, in this life at least, never be adequate to the reality of God, because God is the Mystery that we can never comprehend or understand. The word *God* is only a pointer into that Mystery. God is, as St. Ignatius of Loyola was wont to say, "ever greater" than anything we can grasp or know. In *A Grief Observed* C. S. Lewis notes:

> Images of the Holy easily become holy images—
> sacrosanct. My idea of God is not a divine idea. It
> has to be shattered time after time. He has to shatter
> it Himself. He is the great iconoclast. Could we not
> almost say that this shattering is one of the marks of
> His presence. (1976, 76)

The only thing we can hope for is that our God image
becomes more adequate to the reality of God. How can this
happen? One way is to hear and to read more about God
from theologians and spiritual writers whose own grasp of
God is more adequate to the reality. Many of us need reme-
dial education in God matters. Reading this book, I hope,
will help to change your default image of yourself in relation
with God.

But theological education goes only so far in changing deeply rooted, emotionally charged unconscious patterns.
Something more is needed. I believe that many of us need help
to develop such a trust in God's love for us that we can engage
in a personal relationship with God that will gradually alter
the self-God images that are our defaults. The aim of much of
our religious and spiritual formation, I believe, should be to
help people to develop such a deep trust in God.

The British psychiatrist J. S. McKenzie long ago put
the matter this way:

The *enjoyment of God* should be the supreme end of spiritual technique; and it is in that enjoyment of God that we feel not only saved in the Evangelical sense, but safe: we are conscious of belonging to God, and hence are never alone; and, to the degree we have these two, hostile feelings disappear. . . . In that relationship Nature seems friendly and homely; even its vast spaces instead of eliciting a sense of terror speak of the infinite love; and the nearer beauty becomes the garment with which the Almighty clothes Himself." (cited in Guntrip 1957, 200)

Experiences of the enjoyment of God help to change the default. They also establish a working alliance with God that holds us in the relationship even when we become anxious.

Only when I have a rather firmly established trust in God's love and care for me, a trust based on experiences of God's care and love, can I ask God to reveal my sins and sinful tendencies. No one whose God is a nagging and angry scold would dare to ask God for such a revelation. Those who have formative roles in the church need to take McKenzie's advice seriously, because it is a matter of helping people to have a right relation with God.

Some Ways to Let God Change the Default

As my contribution to this formative work of the church, let me suggest some ways that might allow God a chance to change the default. I often encourage people to contemplate the beauties of nature with the desire to know in their bones God's creative desire that brings everything into existence and keeps it in existence. In the process one can ponder such texts as the creation story of the first chapter of Genesis with its image of God's exuberant joy in all creation and especially in human beings who are made in God's own image and likeness. Or one can ponder this lovely prayer from the book of Wisdom:

> For you love all things that exist,
>> and detest none of the things that you have made,
>> for you would not have made anything if you had hated it.
> How would anything have endured if you had not willed it?
> How would anything not called forth by you have been preserved?
> You spare all things, for they are yours, O Lord,
> you who love the living. (Wisdom 11:24–26)

In Brazil I read this prayer in Portuguese and was deeply moved by the translation of the last words as *amigo da vida*, "friend of life" or "friend of the living." God creates us to be God's friends. Since then I have asked for the grace to let these words sink in so that I more spontaneously react to God as wanting my friendship and enjoying my company. I encourage you to ask God to help you to relish such experiences, to believe them, to let them become your default image of God. What we want and need is to believe and to experience that God likes us, enjoys us, and wants us to enjoy God's presence.

One can take other texts for the same kind of exercise. Some people find it helpful to pray slowly the first eighteen verses of Psalm 139, which begins: "O LORD, you have searched me and known me." To be truthful, with the default most of us have these words can evoke some anxiety. The wagging-finger image can come into play. At least, it did for me when I first began to pray this psalm. But later in the psalm we read: "For it was you who formed my inward parts; / you knit me together in my mother's womb. / I praise you, for I am fearfully and wonderfully made. / Wonderful are your works; / that I know very well" (13–14). People who have persisted in praying this psalm have grown comfortable and trusting in God's presence, so much so that they then can say and mean the last words of the psalm: "Search me, O God, and know my heart; / test me and know my thoughts. / See if there is any wicked way in me, / and lead me in the way everlasting" (23–24). I could say these words honestly and with fervor only when I had come to feel that I was deeply loved and cared for. Then I was surer that God would only reveal my sinful tendencies to help me, not to punish me. Such a result was the fruit of repeated praying of the early parts of the psalm.

Jesus gave us a number of parables that seem aimed at changing the default image of God. One that bears regular contemplation is that of the prodigal son, but that could more aptly be named the "The Prodigally Generous Father" (Luke 15:11–32). The younger son, it seems, cannot turn the father's love away, no matter how low he sinks. In effect, he tells his father, "I wish you were dead!" when he asks for his inheritance. A peasant hearing this story would expect the father to beat the son within an inch of his life. Instead, the father gives him his inheritance, which the son promptly squanders, thus shaming the father even more. Further shame to the father comes when he and the villagers hear that the son now works for a Gentile and feeds the man's pigs. When Jesus' audience hears that the young man is going to come home begging to be treated as a hired hand, they expect that the father will at least beat him, if not kill him, for what he has done. Instead,

Jesus tells them that the father ran through the village to throw his arms around the wastrel and then threw a party for the village. The father even begged the older son to come into the party. In telling this story Jesus is trying to break the default image of God that controls the reactions of his hearers to God, Jesus' own dear Father. Contemplating this parable can change our own default.

The Effects of Prayer on the Default

What these examples suggest is that the default image of self and God is transformed through experiences of God that differ from what the default expects. The process is one of accommodation to the reality of who God is and wants to be for us. As we put ourselves in the way of having such experiences, we may experience some anxiety because the default can be strong. But these new experiences give us the foundation we need to be attracted to exploring the relationship with God in new ways. We come to experience God as desiring our companionship, our friendship, and then we become more willing to continue the exploration of that friendship. The foundational experiences will, it is hoped, forge a strong relationship of trust, a working alliance, as it were, that attracts us to keep coming back to prayer. Gradually, if we continue the process, this new self–God pattern takes precedence in the way we react to God. We have a new default that takes over when we approach prayer.

However, we need to remember that the new pattern is built upon the old one, which remains and to which we can regress in times of inner or outer turmoil or distress. As I noted at the beginning of this chapter, the original default still can take hold of me in spite of years of prayer and study. But after these years I can more easily call upon the experiences that provided a new default and treat the old ways as a temptation.

Spiritual Direction as a Help

In this process of growth toward a new default image of God spiritual directors can be very helpful. Such companions function analogously to a counselor, but the nature of the conversation differs. Spiritual directors focus our conversations with them on what happens when we consciously engage in the relationship with God. Spiritual directors, who are most helpful in the kind of journey I am suggesting, are those who are not authoritarian and directive but who listen well and keep encouraging us to return to the encounter with God. They also help by pointing out the blind alleys we get into and enabling us to see how we got into them. It is not possible within the parameters of this chapter to say more on this topic. I refer readers interested in reading more on spiritual direction to the recommended reading.

Conclusion

We carry the baggage of our upbringing into all our adult relationships, including our relationship with God. Just as the residue of all our past relationships colors our adult relationships with close friends, so too, is our adult relationship with God. The relationships with our friends develop into mutual bonds of trust and challenge through the experience of engaging in them and working through the effects of the residue from past relationships that get in the way. We can move beyond the default self-other patterns formed in childhood by engaging with our friends and suffering the ups and downs entailed in the maturing of any close relationship. So too, with God we can move beyond a default learned in childhood and develop a more mature adult relationship by engaging in the relationship with God. The main reason that we can is that God wants such a mature relationship of friendship to develop. God likes us and wants our friendship. God wants each of us to engage in a relationship of growing intimacy and friendship. If we do, we will find that our default has changed, almost by osmosis.

15

Is God Enough?

In the "Contemplation to Attain Love," the last exercise of the Spiritual Exercises, Ignatius of Loyola proposes this prayer as an appropriate response to our contemplation of all the gifts we have received from God: "Take Lord, and receive all my liberty, my memory, my understanding, all my will—all that I have and possess. You, Lord, have given all that to me. I now give it back to you, O Lord. All of it is yours. Dispose of it according to your will. Give me love of yourself along with your grace, for that is enough for me" (#234).

The St. Louis Jesuits' version of this prayer has people singing: "Give me only your love and your grace; that's enough for me. Your love and your grace are enough for me." Are we serious when we sing these words or when we pray Ignatius's prayer? Is God enough?

The title of this chapter is meant to be provocative, but the question is a serious one. Can we truly say and mean that God *is* enough? Does God want us to come to this point? Some spiritual writing gives the impression that those who are serious about the spiritual life must find God enough, so much so that they need to cut themselves off from all created things, including other people. For example, I found this statement on the Internet from one Carmelite community: "St. Teresa of Ávila says clearly that the desire of the Carmelite is *'to be alone with the Alone.'* God reveals Himself to the heart in solitude, and therefore, each nun works alone, as much as possible, either in her cell or office. There is to be no speaking without necessity outside of the two daily recreations. The strict enclosure, walls and grates separate the religious from the world and help to promote and protect this solitude" (www.sspxasia.com/Documents/Society_of_Saint_Pius_X/ Vocations/Womens-Communities/Chapter-1-Carmel).

Is this what it means to find God enough, to be "alone with the Alone"?

Buddhist spirituality, it seems, advocates the giving up of all desire. Desire, according to the Buddha, is the cause of all human unhappiness; hence, the way to perfection is to strip oneself of all desire. Could this be what it means to find God enough? Some Christian ascetic theory seemed to suggest the necessity of a similar effacement of all desire except the desire for God. Is this what it means to find God enough?

At the beginning of the Spiritual Exercises, Ignatius proposes for consideration the "Principle and Foundation":

> Human beings are created to praise, reverence, and serve God our Lord, and by means of doing this to save their souls.
>
> The other things on the face of the earth are created for the human beings, to help them in the pursuit of the end for which they are created.
>
> From this it follows that we ought to use these things to the extent that they help us toward our end, and free ourselves from them to the extent that they hinder us from it.
>
> To attain this it is necessary to make ourselves *indifferent* to all created things, in regard to everything which is left to our free will and is not forbidden. (#23, italics mine)

Could it be that we find God enough by becoming "indifferent" to everything that is not God?

In the history of spirituality that little word *indifferent* has caused the spillage of a lot of ink and has also provoked some attitudes that seem less than Christlike. The notion of treating a thing or person with indifference sounds rather uncaring, even cold. Modern environmentalists would find in these words of Ignatius the seeds of attitudes that have led to the present plight of our globe.

A Twelve-Step Approach to the Question

I want to approach an answer in a positive way. Let me begin with an example that may seem far afield. Many recovering addicts tell us that they have been saved from addiction to alcohol or drugs or some other substance by admitting that they were helpless with regard to the addiction; turning to a higher power was their only solution. When you listen to the stories of recovering addicts, you realize that in some significant way they are saying that God is enough for them. They had tried any number of other solutions to their addiction, but finally they had to admit that they were indeed helpless, that they were clearly not in control. Thus, they had no other recourse but to turn to a higher power, which many have come to recognize as the Mystery we name God. Without God, they believe and say, they would be dead of the addiction or still in its clutches, and so just as good as dead.

That it was a choice between alcohol and a higher power becomes clear in this statement by a recovering alcoholic: "I would hang on to sobriety for short intervals, but always there would come the tide of an overpowering *necessity* to drink and, as I was engulfed in it, I felt such a sense of panic that I really believed I would die if I didn't get that drink inside" (Alcoholics Anonymous 1976, 306). Notice that alcohol had become her salvation, what she believed in and what, in effect, she worshipped. Then she chose to put her trust in another power, to worship at another altar, and this was enough for her.

But no one in any twelve-step program that I know of would ever say that this radical and absolute dependence on God requires or even tolerates a denial of one's need of other human beings. In fact, almost all the stories in the "Big Book of Alcoholics Anonymous" tell of a frightening aloneness, an almost total loss of connection to other human beings and to one's environment while in the throes of the addiction and before taking the first three steps of the program. What started them on the road to recovery was the help of other addicts who were in recovery and who offered them the hope that they had found in the program and in the fellowship of AA and similar groups. When they embarked on the program, they began to recover their physical, emotional, psychological, and spiritual health and in the process found joy and friendship beyond their wildest expectations.

Here is an example from *The Anonymous Disciple* by Gerard Goggins, a novel about two Jesuits, who were recovering alcoholics. In this scene Jim, the talkative one and the protagonist of the novel, is visited in the hospital late one night by Fred, the other Jesuit. Jim engages in this soliloquy:

> I wonder what kind of man I would be if I was not an alcoholic. I wonder what kind of Jesuit. I'd probably be proud and off the track. I'd have wound up being an apostate or a ladies' man. I would have been a disgrace to the Society. And instead, because I'm an alcoholic and because of A.A. and because of you, Fred, I have found love and peace and fulfillment. I have found friendship, and I have found my vocation even if it's not the one I expected. (1995, 168)

God was absolutely necessary for Jim's sobriety, but God's necessity did not require the loss of all other company. Rather, the opposite; God's necessity seems to have given him back companionship and friendship. This is one clue to the answer to our question.

The Consequences of Idol Worship

In the book of Exodus we hear God saying: "You shall not make for yourself an idol, whether in the form of anything that is in heaven above, or that is on the earth beneath, or that is in the water under the earth. You shall not bow down to them or worship them; for I the LORD your God am a jealous God, punishing children for the iniquity of parents, to the third and the fourth generation of those who reject me, but showing steadfast love to the thousandth generation of those who love me and keep my commandments" (Exodus 20:4–6).

We can read these verses and cringe; or we can read them in the spirit of the freed alcoholic, realizing the truth they contain. The Bible uses human language for an almost impossible task, namely, to tell us who God is and what God wants. To have a dim understanding of this revelation, we must not focus on single texts but try to take in the whole sweep of biblical revelation along with the ways the people of God have experienced and interpreted that sweep over the centuries since it was first written down. The Mystery we call God revealed over this long time, and especially in the life, death, and resurrection of Jesus of Nazareth, cannot be discerned in the image of a jealous human lover.

But human beings have learned, through their folly, the disastrous consequences of worshipping an idol instead of the living God. These consequences play themselves out in individual, familial, and international history. These consequences feel like punishment for the folly, punishment exacted by a jealous God. Hence, the writer of Exodus attributes the consequences of idolatry to God's anger.

In *Holiness, Speech and Silence: Reflections on the Question of God*, Nicholas Lash notes that the word *god* refers to what we worship. Most often we find out who our "god" is in crunch time, as it were. In the trenches of the First World War, John Macmurray came to see that the Christian churches of Europe were worshipping a tribal god, praying to "their" god to give them victory over their and their god's enemies. On a rehab leave back in Great Britain Macmurray was asked to preach at a Sunday service; he spoke of the need for Christians to prepare for the reconciliation of the nations after the war. This Christian audience greeted him with cold hostility; their god was a tribal god. The alcoholic woman mentioned just a moment ago found out that she was worshipping alcohol when she faced the terror of not being able to find another drink.

Once I found that I was worshipping an idol. I had fallen in love, having developed a profound friendship with a woman religious. As a result of her own experiences in her congregation she decided that she no longer belonged in religious life. I supported her decision and thought that I also supported her desire to date and marry. It was fine until she told me that she was falling in love with a man she had begun to date. My heart seemed torn in two; I found myself distraught and deeply pained, unable to focus on other things. I prayed for healing because my better self wanted what was best for her. On one occasion during this time of turmoil I contemplated the story of the two blind men in Matthew 9:27–31. They followed Jesus up to his house, begging for mercy. Then Jesus turned to them and said: "Do you believe that I can do this?" Jesus was talking to me too. I knew immediately that if I said yes I would be healed. But I couldn't say it. If I were healed, I felt, I would lose her friendship. That was too much; I could not ask for healing. The best I could do, and it was, at first, a weak request, was to ask for the desire to be healed. I was, as recovering alcoholics say of themselves while caught in their disease, "insane." It seemed that I could not live without her friendship, an insane idea. In fact the only way I could be her friend was through being healed of this insanity. My heart needed to become what I said it was, a heart committed to religious chastity, a heart committed to a nonexclusive friendship. I was, thank God, freed; I continue to be her friend and a friend to her family.

In *Faith Beyond Resentment* the English theologian James Alison provides another example of the worship of an idol and gives me the words to understand my own past predicament. He was a Dominican priest teaching in a Dominican center in South America. One day the dean called him in to tell him that fourteen religious superiors had written a letter saying that they would not send seminarians to the center as long as Alison was on the faculty. The reason was Alison's activism on gay issues. Without going into the details of what happened, I want to focus on his discovery when he went on a retreat. During this time of prayer he came to see that he was worshipping an idol. He was looking to the hierarchy to tell him that he was OK, not to God. He writes: "In my violent zeal (to win a hearing about homosexuality) I was fighting so that the ecclesiastical structure might speak to me a 'Yes,' a 'Flourish, son,' precisely because I feared that, should I stand alone before God, God himself would be part of the 'do not be.'"(2001, 39).

In other words, God would reject him. He realized that he had despaired of God and had been trying to manipulate church authorities to say that he was OK as a gay man. They would, he hoped, shore up his identity, remove his self-loathing. Now he understood that no human structure, no human being, could do what only God could do. Only God could tell him what he needed to hear to accept himself as a beloved son of God. Finally during this retreat he heard God speak that "profound 'Yes'" to him that he had despaired of ever hearing, that the "little gay boy" was loved by his Father (2001, 39). He concludes by writing, "The 'I', the 'self' of the child of God, is born in the midst of the ruins of repented idolatry" (2001, 40).

Alison gives me words to understand what had happened to me, and possibly what happens to anyone who comes to believe that he or she needs someone or something to feel whole, to be someone. Ultimately, only God can do this for us. Nothing else will suffice to give us ourselves.

Self-Knowledge in Crunch Times

In crunch times we become aware of the truth about ourselves, and the truth is often devastating. We realize that we have been worshipping idols. This realization, however, comes as a great grace, not a disaster. Now we can pray and mean that great prayer of the New Testament, "I believe; help my unbelief" (Mark 9:24). To the extent that we believe in God, to that extent we are free and whole and loving. To that extent we have the "hundredfold." But the only way to that hundredfold lies through the darkness of giving up our idols, those persons or things that, deep down, we believe we cannot live without.

Notice, also, that there is a way in which this death to idols can seem like losing everything else; it feels as though our situation after we have given up the idols will be to be all alone, or even more frightening, to be no one. Why? Because we are using these idols to shore up our identity. Who we are seems tied up with them. Moreover, until the scales are torn from our eyes, it does seem as though we cannot exist without them. It seems that God is demanding that we surrender all that we are and have and that we will then be "alone with the Alone," indeed. In addition, as

Alison makes clear, to give up our idols means to live with the consequences of being defenseless in a hostile and violent world.

The Example of Jesus

But, is this not just what Jesus did? Jesus lived in this world as a human being without idols, as the kind of human being God intends in creating us in God's own image and likeness. As such, Jesus becomes the victim of the violence unleashed by a world that cannot see any other way to be human except to live in constant fear of the other, whoever that other may be.

So we come close to grasping how God is enough through experiencing what happens when we try to forge our own identity through idolatrous means. The story of Adam and Eve is a paradigm of our human situation. They are created in the image and likeness of God and enjoy all the bounties of the garden of delights. They want for nothing, it seems. But they are tempted. If they eat of the forbidden tree, they are told, they will become like God. Notice that they already have, by gift and grace, what the tempter tells them they will grab by eating; they are, by God's creative gift, made in the image and likeness of God. As such, they will, in some way, live forever because God desires them into existence. They exist because God wants them, and God's desire is the only guarantee they have of living forever. But they come to believe that they can gain control over their existence, become like God, by eating the forbidden fruit. Do you see the subtle point here? They already have, by God's gracious gift, what they now want to have by their own effort, their own will. It is insanity, indeed, to think that they can control life, can become like God by anything they do. Yet they go ahead and act insanely, just as all of us addicts and idolaters have done over the centuries.

A character in P. D. James's detective novel *Devices and Desires* says: "We need, all of us, to be in control of our lives, and so we shrink them until they're small and mean enough so that we can feel in control (1990, 248)." This is what happens when we, like Adam and Eve, act insanely or irrationally. It is insane or irrational to act as though we were or could be in control of our lives; it is irrational to act contrary to the way the world really is. But the world and all that makes it up is, in actuality, contingent, dependent at every moment on the gracious desire of God that it exist. Existence is gift. If we do not accept this basic truth, and I mean accept it in our hearts and bones and flesh, we are living irrationally. The world and all of us who are in it exist by God's gracious desire, not by necessity. Moreover, we are desired into existence because God wants us, not because we are necessary to God. We are desired into existence so that we can freely accept God's friendship, God's love. To be human is to be created by God's desire; and God desires our friendship.

How God Is Enough

There is a hole in each of our hearts. We are made for God's friendship, and nothing else will satisfy us because nothing else will satisfy God. As Augustine wrote in his *Confessions*, we are all made for God, and our hearts are restless until they rest in God. God is enough in this sense: God is the deepest desire of our hearts; nothing else but God will satisfy this desire; and, without God, nothing else will be of any ultimate use to slake our deepest thirst. God is enough to satisfy this thirst. But the paradox is that when we are one with God we can enjoy everything and everyone else nonpossessively.

In a nutshell, then, God is enough because only God will satisfy our deepest desire. But when we are one with God, then we have everything else because God is the creator of everything and everyone and is not niggardly but abundant, exuberant generosity. However, to live in this free way we have to be willing to give up the illusion that we can hold on to anything or anyone by our own efforts; we have to be willing to lose everything and trust that God will provide everything we need.

I hope that I have been pointing toward God, that what I have written makes orthodox sense and that it gives an orthodox and true, even if obscure, understanding of what it means to be "alone with the Alone," of how God can be understood as a jealous God. Only by letting go can we have it all. But this is not the arbitrary demand of a jealous lover; rather, it is the way the world is: bountiful gift. When we are freed of illusion, we can say and mean: "Take Lord, and receive all my liberty, my memory, my understanding, all my will—all that I have and possess. You, Lord, have given all that to me. I now give it back to you, O Lord. All of it is yours. Dispose of it according to your will. Give me love of yourself along with your grace, for that is enough for me" (*Spiritual Exercises*, #234).

"Your love and your grace are enough for me."

16

A Meditation on Death and Life

"Whenever it is a damp, drizzly November in my soul"—these words, in the opening sentence of *Moby Dick*, strike a responsive chord in those of us who live in northern climes. We know how bleak November days can be. For us it seems natural to celebrate the feasts of All Saints and All Souls in November and to complete the liturgical calendar near the end of this month or at the beginning of December. I have often wondered how the liturgical calendar fares in the Southern Hemisphere where November is the heart of spring. Be that as it may be, the November weather and its feast days do face us with the end of life and with thoughts of the end of the world. I wrote this meditation in late November one year. I believe that the message is appropriate even if you use it for meditation at a different time of year.

In his Pulitzer Prize–winning book *The Denial of Death*, Ernest Becker says, "the idea of death, the fear of it, haunts the human animal like nothing else; it is a mainspring of human activity—activity designed largely to avoid the fatality of death, to overcome it by denying in some way that it is the final destiny for man" (1973, ix). He then goes on to argue that this denial is so pervasive—and pernicious—that it is the source of our modern psychic and social ills. He makes a very good case for his argument.

What We Fear with Death

Death faces us with annihilation, the loss of self and all that gives meaning to life. What I fear depends, of course, on what I see as myself. If I am my body, then I will do everything to preserve it. Is this fear behind the cult of the body in our culture? If I am my family or race, then I will do everything to preserve them. In the twentieth century we saw the horrors to which a cult of family or race or country can lead. Rather than explore these different ways of defining the self, I would like to assume that to be a person is to be in relationship, that the unit of the personal is the I and the you.

Without some you, I am not a person. In other words, I need some you to be myself. To get an inkling of the truth of this statement, recall how we cling to important relationships even when these relationships are destructive or when the clinging is destructive. If this statement is true, then what I most fear in dying is the loss of all relationships, which would be the equivalent to the annihilation of myself. Thus, the fear of death is fear of self-annihilation.

Yet to be human is to die. Someone may argue, however, that death entered the world of the human only with sin. Some modern theologians would say that sin did not bring death into the world; rather, sin changed the way we experience death. This is, for example, the argument of Sebastian Moore, OSB, in *Let This Mind Be in You*. In other words, because of sin, we experience death—which is human destiny, part of what it means to be human—as the threat of annihilation. In this understanding, God created human beings whose reality included dying. Hence, death is not annihilation but the final consummation of life and an opening to more life. Death, then, is not the loss of all relationships, but an opening to much wider and deeper relationships. Sin makes the experience dreadful, not creation itself.

The Death of Jesus

To get a purchase on this notion, let us look at the death of Jesus. Jesus, as the sinless one, had no illusions, no rationalizations. He had no progeny as he faced death. He could intuit the doom that faced his people from the Romans, so he could not comfort himself with the triumph of his race. He was betrayed by one of his closest friends, denied by another, and abandoned by all. His body was stripped of all dignity; crucifixion was a horrible way to die. His mission was a failure because he had not convinced his people that he was the Messiah. He was mocked and derided by Jews and Romans alike. Even his Father seemed distant as he cried out: "My God, my God, why have you forsaken me?" (Matthew 27:46). The universe seems to hold its breath. Will Jesus accept what J. R. R. Tolkien calls the "doom of men" willingly, with trust and love? Or will he finally despair? Luke's Gospel seems to capture this feeling: "It was now about noon, and darkness came over the whole land until three in the afternoon, while the sun's light failed; and the curtain of the temple was torn in two" (Luke 23:44–45). One can sense the sigh of relief of the universe as Jesus called out with a loud voice: "Father, into your hands I commend my spirit" (Luke 23:46) and breathed his last.

Sebastian Moore speaks of the chosen passion, not in the sense that Jesus as the sinless one did not have to die, but rather in the sense that Jesus trustingly accepted human destiny. He trusted that God is his Abba ("dear Father," "dear Mother") and that not even death could change who God is. If God is, for all eternity, our Abba, then Jesus and we will be for all eternity God's sons and daughters. Thus, Jesus was the most fully human person who ever lived because he accepted with trust and love the full reality of being human, which included accepting the truth that death is the only way to be fully human. Jesus trusted that he would always be a person even through death, that he would always be in relationship. In fact, only through death could he be more a person, in more relationships, deeper and stronger relationships, not only with Abba but also with all of his brothers and sisters who had gone before him and would come after him.

Perhaps we can now understand better the profound meaning of these words in John's Gospel:

> The hour has come for the Son of Man to be glorified. Very truly I tell you, unless a grain of wheat falls to the ground and dies, it remains just a single grain; but if it dies, it bears much fruit. Those who love their life lose it, and those who hate their life in this world will keep it for eternal life. Whoever serves me must follow me; and where I am, there will my servant be also. Whoever serves me, the Father will honor.
>
> Now my soul is troubled. And what should I say—"Father, save me from this hour"? No, it is for this reason that I have come to this hour. Father, glorify your name. (John 12:23–28)

The only way that Jesus can live, that is, be more fully a person, be glorified, is to die. So in a real sense he does, contrary to Dylan Thomas's advice, "go gentle into that good night." He does choose death.

The Disciples of Jesus

For the disciples, of course, the crucifixion was the shipwreck of all their hopes. We can hear the pathos in the words of the two disciples who met the stranger on the road to Emmaus: "But we had hoped that he was the one to redeem Israel" (Luke 24:21). They had lost the one you who gave meaning to their I. With him gone, who were they? Yet in this very moment of despair something happens that makes their hearts burn within them. Could it be? Whatever it was, they did not want to let this stranger out of their company, and they prevailed on him to stay and eat with them. They felt all the old stirrings of life and warmth and challenge and hope that—could it be?—they had felt in Jesus' presence. "When he was at the table with them, he took bread, blessed and broke it, and gave it to them. Then their eyes were opened, and they recognized him; and he vanished from their sight" (Luke 24:30–31). With this experience they had themselves back, as it were. The one You who made all the difference to who they are is alive and well.

And the vital importance of these first witnesses for us is that they testify that they are experiencing the same Jesus with whom they had walked and talked and ate, the same Jesus whom they had abandoned or denied, the same Jesus whom they had seen die so horribly. Thus, they assure us that the Jesus whom we experience in prayer, in reading the Gospels, in the sacrament of reconciliation, in the Eucharist, is Jesus of Nazareth, Mary's son.

The Heart of the Matter for Us

For that is the heart of the matter when times are dark, when there "is a damp, drizzly November" in our souls. Our hearts do burn within us at times. We do sense the presence of the mysterious other whom we name Jesus, and we know with faith and hope and love, at least in those moments, that death has no sting. In those moments we have no doubts either that it is right for the church to celebrate the feast of All Saints because we know that no one who has died in Christ is lost, annihilated. Rather, we know that "we are surrounded by so great a cloud of witnesses" (Hebrews 12:1) and that we have even more relationships than we could ever count. In those moments, too, we know that it is right for the church to celebrate the feast of All Souls, because we can hope that all our loved ones are, like Mary, in Christ and, therefore, whole and entire and in relationship with us and everyone else. Indeed, it may be a measure of our faith and hope that we pray to (that is, converse with) not only

Jesus, Mary, and the saints but also those of our loved ones who have gone before us into that good night.

Because we have experiences of God the Father, of Jesus, of the Spirit, of Mary, of the saints, and of our loved ones who are saints, we can say with St. Paul:

> What then are we to say about these things? If God is for us, who is against us? He who did not withhold his own Son, but gave him up for all of us, will he not with him also give us everything else? Who will bring any charge against God's elect? It is God who justifies. Who is to condemn? It is Christ Jesus, who died, yes, who was raised, who is at the right hand of God, who indeed intercedes for us. Who will separate us from the love of Christ? Will hardship, or distress, or persecution, or famine, or nakedness, or peril, or sword? As it is written, "For your sake we are being killed all day long; we are accounted as sheep to be slaughtered." No, in all these things we are more than conquerors through him who loved us. For I am convinced that neither death, nor life, nor angels, nor rulers, nor things present, nor things to come, nor powers, nor height, nor depth, nor anything else in all creation, will be able to separate us from the love of God in Christ Jesus our Lord. (Romans 8:31–39)

Perhaps at such times we can even say that death is not the doom of humankind but our boon. For only death will take away the blinders that keep us from experiencing the whole of our reality, that we are in communion with all human beings because we are in communion with the eternal community, Father, Son, and Spirit, the one mystery we call God.

17

To Forgive as Jesus Forgives

I wrote this chapter after reading the 1985 work "Prayer of Forgiveness: The Pain of Intimacy" by the since-deceased Jesuit David Hassel. I wanted to underscore the depth of his insight into forgiveness. My main focus is the forgiveness of those close to us who have hurt us.

Often enough we think it rather heroic if we can refrain from exacting an eye for an eye from those who offend us. And, truth to tell, the world would be a far better place if we humans were capable of this much forgiveness. But when we pray (and mean), "Forgive us our trespasses as we forgive those who trespass against us," we would hardly be satisfied if God were merely to refrain from exacting an eye for an eye. We want more from God than such cold comfort, and in fact, God offers us more. The subtitle of Hassel's essay discloses the key to the mystery of forgiveness; he writes of the "pain of intimacy."

The Way God Forgives

When the prodigal son (Luke 15:11–32) returns to his father's house, the best he hopes for is that his father will let him be a hired servant. Then, at least, he will not be hungry and degraded as he is in the "far country" where he has to tend pigs. The father, however, restores him to the bosom of the family. It is clear from the story that the father does not forget what the prodigal son has done; it seems likely from his conversation with the elder son, for example, that the prodigal's wasted inheritance will not be restored. But the father rejoices in having a son back, not in getting a new hired servant. We sinners have probably rejoiced at the realization that God treats us in this way, too; in spite of our sins, God welcomes us back into the family.

The way Jesus deals with Peter in John 21 offers another example. Jesus does not just tell Peter that he will not hold his denial against him. He does far more; he invites Peter back into intimate friendship and asks him to take care of others. Many Christians, identifying with Peter, have been overwhelmed with wonder and happiness to realize that Jesus offers them intimate friendship and companionship on mission, even after they have offended him deeply.

These two Gospel stories underline what Christ's for-giveness really means. Jesus does not merely not retaliate in kind; he goes beyond not holding a grudge. He takes us back into intimate friendship where we can hurt him once again. Moreover, he entrusts us with responsibilities for others' well-being and even their salvation in spite of the fact that he knows our weak characters. It is the kind of forgiveness that leads to a desire in us to be the kind of people he seems to believe we can be. But it does not make it impossible for us to fail him again. Moreover, we experience time and again that we do fail him again. Nevertheless he offers us this kind of intimacy. This is how Jesus forgives us.

The New Commandment

In the last discourse in John's Gospel (13–17) Jesus is heard to say a number of times and in different ways: "I give you a new commandment, that you love one another. Just as I have loved you, you also should love one another" (John 13:34). In the moment of accepting his forgiveness we may see with rather blinding clarity that we, too, are called to forgive in the same way. If the emotion of the moment does not render us insensible, we will recognize the enormity of the demand on our hearts.

Some examples poignantly and powerfully make the point, such as the rape victim who feels challenged to forgive the one who violated her, or the father called to forgive the killer of his son. We may recoil in anger and resentment from such a demand. We may want to throw up our hands in despair, aware of how limited and unforgiving our hearts are and of how complex human situations of hurt and forgiveness can be. We cannot forgive as Jesus forgives, it seems. For to forgive the one who has hurt us means to make ourselves vulnerable to the same hurt again. Only a fool would take such a chance. What can we do?

What We Can Do

The love commandment is an impossible one for human hearts and wills to bring off. All we can do is to desire to love as Jesus loves and to ask the help of his Spirit to do so. So too, with forgiveness. We cannot, of ourselves, forgive as he forgives, that is, invite back into intimacy those who have hurt and offended us. But we can desire to forgive in this way. Moreover, we can expect to resist that desire just as strongly as we resist the desire to love as Jesus loves. Still let us recall the words Paul heard: "My grace is sufficient for you, for power is made perfect in weakness" (2 Corinthians 12:9). We, too, can hope that God's grace will do what seems impossible for us.

But it takes time. We need to be patient with ourselves and also persevering in asking the Lord's help to continue to desire to forgive. One heartfelt prayer for the grace to forgive is often not enough to heal all our hurt, touch all the dimensions of our relationship to the one who has hurt us. For one thing, we need to be aware that a heartfelt desire to forgive can just as well coexist with a reluctance to do so, as, for example, a heartfelt desire for closeness to God can coexist with a strong fear of such closeness and, therefore, with a resistance to it. Ambivalence is, it seems, the characteristic state of the human heart. We can love and hate the same person, desire to forgive and desire not to forgive, seemingly at the same moment. Jesus knows how complex our motivation can be; if he still loves us and is patient with us, then perhaps we can be more patient with ourselves—but also persevering in asking his help to overcome the ambivalence.

Second, we need to take into account the lag time between the heartfelt desire to forgive and our emotional ability to do so. Often enough people are troubled by the fact that they still feel resentful even though they have consciously chosen to forgive as Jesus forgives. For instance, a close friend deeply offended you by believing a story about you that was untrue. You have confronted him, and he has expressed his sorrow and asked your forgiveness. You want to forgive him and resume the friendship, and you even say that you do forgive him. You ask Jesus for help to forgive. But periodically you recall the hurt and feel angry and resentful and mistrustful all over again. Does this not mean that deep down you have not really forgiven him? It can be quite disheartening to find that these feelings recur.

Perhaps we can be helped by a concept borrowed from psychoanalysis. In the course of psychotherapy a client may have a breakthrough insight into both the cause and effects of a certain type of self-defeating behavior. The client may feel freed of the dynamic that leads to such behavior as a result of the insight. It is often disheartening to clients when they find themselves once again acting in the self-defeating pattern. Psychoanalysts speak of the need to work through the insight. That is, the insight must be allowed to permeate the various layers of the psyche, and this happens only slowly and with much reluctance and resistance. The client is helped to persevere in the working through by the persistence of the analyst and by the memory of the freeing experience of having the insight.

So too, it seems to me, a sense of freedom and wholeness and relief accompanies the desire to forgive. But it does not all at once permeate all of our desires and feelings. The spirit of forgiveness must be allowed time to penetrate all the layers of myself and especially that layer that seems to want to hug hurts and never let them go. For this penetration to happen I need both patience and perseverance, patience with the slowness of the process, and perseverance in asking the Spirit's help in allowing that spirit of forgiveness to do its work.

The breakthrough that leads to the desire to forgive a friend who has hurt you is often accompanied by a great relief, a lifting of spirits, a joy that you will have your friend once again. But periodically, especially when you are down or in a depressed mood, you experience the resentment all over again. You wonder whether your friend recognizes how much you suffered from his suspicion of you. Self-pity surfaces and has a chance to be healed if we talk with Jesus about these feelings also. At another time the friend may ask a favor, and you feel that he has a nerve asking you to put yourself out after what he did. Each of these eruptions of the resentment gives us a chance to work through, or better, to let the Spirit of forgiveness work through our whole being to make us more and more like Jesus.

Once again we return to the need to trust in the power of God's grace to do what seems impossible. It is a measure of our megalomania, but also of our helplessness, that we often feel that even the grace of God cannot overcome our resistance to love and to forgive as Jesus loves and forgives. We need to ask for faith in a God who says, "My grace is sufficient for you" (2 Corinthians 12:9).

18

Humbled

I wrote this meditation on humility at the request of the editors of *America* as part of their Lenten series for 2006. It seems to be a fitting way to end this series of meditations on the effects of prayer.

I don't want to be humbled; you don't either, I suspect. Yet there are people who say that being humbled was the best thing that ever happened to them. Members of Alcoholics Anonymous, for example, say that they only began to move toward sanity and wholeness when they were deeply humbled. Some elderly people discover happiness and peace when they come to accept being humbled by the aging process. What could that mean?

Paul says of Jesus, "He humbled himself and became obedient to the point of death—even death on a cross," a punishment the Romans used to show who was boss (Philippians 2:8). Paul indicates that in Jesus God "emptied himself." We tend to think of God as unchanging, untouchable, all powerful. But let's take seriously what Paul says about God in Jesus. God, then, is the vulnerable one, the one who does not stand on rights and dignity and honor but who empties self to come close and to engage us. God is that vulnerable, vulnerable enough to die on the cross to win our friendship.

We are created in the image and likeness of God; perhaps, then, to be human means to be vulnerable and to recognize how vulnerable we are. This would mean to accept the reality that we do not have control over our lives in any but a superficial sense. We exist only because God wants us. It is, however, difficult for us to keep the conviction that everything we are and have is always gift. We want to be invulnerable and tend to believe that we are in control or should be. We glory in our talents, our achievements, our successes. In our hearts we are like the Pharisee who thanked God that he was not like other people, and then went on to list how he differed from them, and especially from the publican (Luke 18:9–14). Sometimes we come to our senses and realize that all is gift, but it is hard to hold on to that truth.

Perhaps, then, some of us need to be humbled in order to lose our arrogance and our belief that we have control of life. This, it seems, is what happens when an addict hits bottom. The choices are stark: to continue trying to control one's life with the bottle and thus spiraling down the black hole to oblivion and death or to admit one's helplessness and to ask God's help. Many addicts say that they needed to be humbled to begin to move toward sanity and life. In addition, only when they had lost everything and turned to God for help did they come gradually to realize that God loves them drunk or sober, a success or a failure, but wants their wholeness, sanity, and friendship, which they can only have if they are sober.

I live at an infirmary and nursing home for elderly and sick Jesuits. So I see men who have been humbled by the aging process. Perhaps all of us need practice in being humbled to prepare for old age, sickness, and death. At that time we may well find ourselves unable to take care of ourselves, needing help to eat, go to the bathroom, and take a shower or bath. Humbled indeed, you might say. More and more of us can, however, look forward to this kind of life. When we are humbled in this way, we may find ourselves full of anger and self-pity, railing at fate, at people who forced us to go to a nursing home, at God, a not wholly inappropriate first response. Some people, however, never move beyond this stage and live the rest of their lives with anger, resentment, and bitterness. But those who come to terms with what has happened, gradually realize how blessed they are to have lived at all and to be still alive; they often experience great happiness and contentment.

As I noted earlier, the psychoanalyst Erik Erikson defined the last stage of the life cycle as the struggle between wisdom and despair. Despair means the refusal or inability to accept who I am now with all that has gone into making me who I am. Wisdom means the acceptance of the one life cycle I had as the only one possible. To believe that God wants my friendship now in spite of my sins and failings is to be truly wise and deeply happy. I believe that those who have been humbled and who come to live with some joy and élan have that kind of wisdom. They can even say of their sins and failures that they were happy faults. Many of us only come to this kind of wisdom when we are humbled, and we thank God for that grace. But I'm still leery of being humbled, and, I suspect, you are too. But we can pray for the grace to accept the humiliations life brings and to trust God's words to Paul, "My grace is sufficient for you" (2 Corinthians 12:9).

Recommended Reading

On Prayer

Barry, William A. *A Friendship Like No Other: Experiencing God's Amazing Embrace*. Chicago: Loyola Press, 2008.

———. *God and You: Prayer as a Personal Relationship*. New York: Paulist Press, 1987.

———. *Paying Attention to God: Discernment in Prayer*. Notre Dame, IN: Ave Maria Press, 1990.

———. *What Do I Want in Prayer?* New York: Paulist Press, 1994.

———. *With an Everlasting Love: Developing an Intimate Relationship with God*. New York: Paulist Press, 1999.

Coffey, Kathy. *God in the Moment: Making Every Day a Prayer*. Chicago: Loyola Press, 2005.

Green, Thomas. *Opening to God*. Notre Dame, IN: Ave Maria Press, 2008.

———. *When the Well Runs Dry*. Notre Dame, IN: Ave Maria Press, 1998.

Silf, Margaret. *Inner Compass: An Invitation to Ignatian Spirituality*. Chicago: Loyola Press, 2007.

Thibodeaux, Mark. *Armchair Mystic: Easing into Contemplative Prayer*. Cincinnati, OH: St. Anthony Messenger, 2001.

On Discernment and the Examination of Consciousness

Barry, William A. *What Do I Want in Prayer?* New York: Paulist Press, 1994. (See especially appendix B.)

Hamm, Dennis. "Rummaging for God: Praying Backward through Your Day." *America*, May 14, 1994, 22–23.

On Spiritual Direction

Barry, William A., and William J. Connolly. *The Practice of Spiritual Direction*. San Francisco: HarperOne, 1982. (A revised edition is forthcoming.)

Seek and Find Guide: A Worldwide Resource Guide for Available Spiritual Directors. Spiritual Directors International, http://www.sdiworld.org. (For names of spiritual directors in your area.)

References

Alcoholics Anonymous. *Alcoholics Anonymous: The Story of How Many Thousands of Men and Women Have Recovered from Alcoholism,* 3rd ed. New York: Alcoholics Anonymous World Services, 1976. (Commonly known as *The Big Book*.)

Alison, James. *Faith Beyond Resentment: Fragments Catholic and Gay.* New York: Crossroad, 2001.

———. *The Joy of Being Wrong: Original Sin through Easter Eyes.* New York: Crossroad, 1998.

Augustine, Saint. *Confessions.* Tr. R. S. Pine-Coffin. Hammondsworth, England: Penguin Books, 1961.

Becker, Ernest. *The Denial of Death.* New York: The Free Press, 1973.

Blevins, Win. *Stone Song: A Novel of the Life of Crazy Horse.* New York: Tom Doherty Associates, 1995.

Buechner, Frederick. *The Sacred Journey.* San Francisco: Harper & Row, 1982.

Documents of the Thirty-Fourth General Congregation of the Society of Jesus. St. Louis, MO: Institute of Jesuit Sources, 1995.

Erikson, Erik. *Childhood and Society.* Second Edition, Revised and Enlarged. New York: W. W. Norton, 1963.

Goggins, Gerard. *The Anonymous Disciple.* Worcester, MA: Assumption Publications, 1995.

Guntrip, Henry. *Psychotherapy and Religion.* New York: Harper, 1957.

Hassel, David, SJ. *Review for Religious,* 44 (1985): 388–97.

James, P. D. *Devices and Desires.* New York: Alfred A. Knopf, 1990.

Julian of Norwich. *Revelations of Divine Love. (Short Text and Long Text).* Tr. Elizabeth Spearing. London, New York: Penguin Books, 1998.

Lash, Nicholas. *Holiness, Speech and Silence: Reflections on the Question of God.* Burlington, VT: Ashgate, 2005.

Leech, Kenneth. *Experiencing God: Theology as Spirituality.* New York: Harper and Row, 1985.

Levertov, Denise. *The Stream and the Sapphire: Selected Poems on Religious Themes.* New York: New Directions, 1997.

Lewis, C. S. *A Grief Observed.* New York: Bantam Books, 1976.

Lindbergh, Anne Morrow. *Gift from the Sea.* New York: Vintage Books, 1965.

Macmurray, John. *Persons in Relation.* Atlantic Highlands, NJ: Humanities Press, 1961.

Malone, Matt. "The Father of Mercies," *America,* March 7, 2005.

Meissner, William. *Ignatius of Loyola: The Psychology of a Saint.* New Haven, CT: Yale University Press, 1992.

Moore, Brian. *Black Robe.* New York: Plume, 1997.

Moore, Sebastian. *Let This Mind Be in You: The Quest for Identity through Oedipus to Christ.* Minneapolis: Winston, 1985.

O'Connor, Flannery. "Revelation." *The Complete Stories.* New York: Farrar, Straus and Giroux, 1987.

Stark, Rodney. *The Rise of Christianity: How the Obscure, Marginal Jesus Movement Became the Dominant Religious Force in the Western World in a Few Centuries.* San Francisco: HarperCollins, 1997.

Tutu, Desmond. *No Future without Forgiveness.* New York: Doubleday Image, 1999.

Tyler, Anne. *Dinner at the Homesick Restaurant.* New York: Ballantine Books, 1996.

Williams, Rowan. *On Christian Theology.* Oxford: Blackwell, 2000.

Wright, N. T. *The Challenge of Jesus: Rediscovering Who Jesus Was and Is.* Downers Grove, IL: InterVarsity Press, 1999.

———. "How Jesus Saw Himself." *Bible Review,* 12, no. 3 (1996): 29.

Young, William J., comp. and trans. *Letters of St. Ignatius of Loyola.* Chicago: Loyola University Press, 1959.